GREAT BRITAIN IN YOUR POCKET

GREAT BRITAIN IN YOUR POCKET

A STEP-BY-STEP GUIDE
AND TRAVEL ITINERARY

BY RICK STEVES

Northcote House

British Library Cataloguing in Publication Data

Steves, Rick, 1955-

Great Britain in your pocket: a step-by-step guide and travel itinerary.—UK ed.—(Pocket travellers).
1. Great Britain—Visitors' guides.
I. Title II. Steves, Rick, *1955*- Great Britain in 22 days III. Series
914.1'04858

ISBN 1-85373-095-5

© 1986, 1987 by Rick Steves
UK edition © 1988 by Northcote House Publishers

Maps Dave Hoerlein

All rights reserved. No part of this work may be reproduced, other than for purposes of review, without the express permission of the Publishers given in writing.

This edition first published in 1988 by Northcote House Publishers Ltd, Harper & Row House, Estover Road, Plymouth PL6 7PZ, United Kingdom. Tel: Plymouth (0752) 705251. Telex: 45635. Fax: (0752) 777603.

Made and printed in Great Britain by
Richard Clay Ltd, Bungay, Suffolk

CONTENTS

How to Use This Book 7
Back Door Travel Philosophy 14
Itinerary 15
Tour 1 Fly to London 20
Tour 2 Around London 30
Tour 3 More of London 36
Tour 4 Salisbury, Stonehenge, Bath 38
Tour 5 Bath 40
Tour 6 Wells, Glastonbury, Wookey Hole 44
Tour 7 South Wales, Folk Museum, Wye River Valley 46
Tour 8 Cotswold Villages, Blenheim Palace 50
Tour 9 Stratford, Warwick Castle, Coventry Cathedral 54
Tour 10 Ironbridge Gorge, North Wales 58
Tour 11 Exploring North Wales 63
Tour 12 Blackpool, England's Playground 65
Tour 13 Lake District 69
Tour 14 Exploring the Lake District 73
Tour 15 Lake District to West Coast of Scotland 75
Tour 16 Highlands, Loch Ness, Scenic Drive 79
Tour 17 Edinburgh 82
Tour 18 Edinburgh 87
Tour 19 Hadrian's Wall, Durham 91
Tour 20 North York Moors, York 94
Tour 21 York 97
Tour 22 York, Cambridge, London 99
Post-Tour Option Ireland 103
Practical Extras
  Sleeping 108
  Eating 109
  Money 111
  Driving 111
  This Tour by Train and Coach 113
  Festivals 117
Cultural Insights for Travellers
  What's so Great About Britain 118
  History 119
  Architecture 121
  British TV 123
  Telephoning 124
  Weights & Measures 126

Great Britain

HOW TO USE THIS BOOK

This book is the tour guide in your pocket. It lets you be the boss by giving you the best basic itinerary in Britain and a suggested way to use that time most efficiently.

Great Britain in Your Pocket is for do-it-yourselfers who would like the organisation and smoothness of a tour without the straight-jacket. It's almost having your cake and eating it too.

This series originated (and is still used) as hand-books for those who join me on my 'Back Door Europe' tours. Since most large organised tours work to keep their masses ignorant while visiting many of the same places we'll cover, this book is handy for anyone taking a typical big coach tour — but wanting also to maintain some independence and flexibility.

This plan is maximum thrills per mile, minute and pound. It's designed for travel by hired car, but is adaptable to train (see 'Practical Extras' in the back of this book). The pace is fast but not hectic and is designed for the visitor with limited time who wants to see everything but doesn't want the 'if it's Tuesday this must be Edinburgh' craziness. The plan includes the predictable 'required' biggies (Big Ben, Stratford, Wordsworth's cottage and Stonehenge) with a good dose of 'Back Door' intimacy — cosy Cotswold villages, windswept Roman lookouts, Gaelic folk pubs, angelic boys' choirs — mixed in.

Great Britain in Your Pocket is balanced and streamlined, avoiding typical tourist burn-out by including only the most exciting castles and churches. I've been very selective. For example, we won't visit both Oxford and Cambridge — just the best of the two. The 'best', of course, is only my opinion. But after ten busy years of travel writing, lecturing and tour guiding, I've developed a sixth sense of what tickles the traveller's fancy. I love this itinerary. I get excited just thinking about it.

Of course, connect-the-dots travel isn't perfect, just as colour-by-number painting isn't good art. But this book is your smiling Scotsman, your Bobbie in a jam, your handbook. It's your well-thought-out and tested itinerary. I've done it — and refined it — many times on my own and with groups. Use it, take advantage of it, but don't let it rule you.

Read this book before you begin your trip. Use it as a rack to hang more ideas on. As you plan and study and travel and talk to people, you'll fill this book with notes. It's your tool. The book is completely modular and is adaptable to any trip. You'll find 22 units (tours) — or days — each built with the same sections:

1. **Introductory overview** for the day.
2. An hour-by-hour **Suggested schedule** recommended for that

day.
3. List of the most important **Sightseeing highlights** (rated:
● ● ● Don't miss; ● ● Try hard to see; ● Worthwhile if you can make it).
4. **Transport** tips and instructions.
5. **Food** and **accommodation**: How and where to find the best budget places, including addresses, phone numbers, and my favourites.
6. **Orientation** and an easy-to-read **map** locating all recommended places.
7. **Helpful hints** on shopping, transport, day-to-day chores.
8. **Itinerary options** for those with more or less than the suggested time, or with particular interests. This itinerary is *rubbery!*

At the end of the book you'll find special chapters on such things as English history and politics, post-tour options, tips on telephoning, car hire, driving, etc.

Travel smart

This itinerary assumes you are a well-organised traveller who lays departure groundwork upon arrival in a town, reads a day ahead in this book, uses a larger directory-type guidebook and the local tourist info offices, and enjoys the hospitality of the British people. Ask questions. Most locals are eager to point you in their idea of the right direction. Use the telephone, wear a moneybelt, use a small pocket notebook to organise your thoughts and make simplicity a virtue. If you insist on being confused, your trip will be a mess. If you expect yourself to travel smart, you will.

Cost

This trip's cost breaks down like this: The cost of getting to London, which will vary according to where you start from. A three-week car hire (split between two people, including tax, insurance and petrol) or three weeks of rail and bus travel—£300 ($525). For room and board work on £18 ($30) a day, double occupancy—around £380 ($660). This is more than feasible, and if necessary, you can travel cheaper (see *Europe Through the Back Door* for the skills and tricks of travelling cheap). Add £120-£175 ($200-$300) fun money and you've got yourself a great British adventure for under £900 ($1,600), plus the cost of travelling to London.

When to go

July and August are peak season—best weather and the fullest schedule of tourist fun, but very crowded, most difficult, and

How to Use This Book

more expensive. Most of us travel during this period, and this book tackles peak season problems, especially that of finding a room.

'Off-peak' travel (May, early June, September, and early October) is ideal. If at all possible, plan an off-peak trip for minimal crowds, decent weather, sights and tourist fun spots still open, and the joy of being able to just grab a room almost whenever and wherever you like.

Winter travellers find absolutely no crowds, but many sights and accommodation are closed or run on a severely limited schedule. The weather can be cold and dreary, and nightfall will draw curtains on your sightseeing well before dinner time.

In my experience, British weather is reliably unpredictable (but mostly bad) and July and August are not much better than off-peak months. Septembers are often lovely. Conditions can change several times in a day but rarely is the weather extreme. Daily averages through the spring, summer and autumn months range between 42 and 70 degrees, and temperatures below 32 or over 80 are cause for headlines.

Prices and times

Prices for major items are shown but I haven't cluttered this book with many minor prices (eg specific admission fees and student discounts etc). Small charges of less than a pound shouldn't affect your sightseeing decisions.

Prices as well as opening hours, telephone numbers, and so on, are always changing and I've tossed timidity out the window, knowing you'll understand that this book, like any guidebook, starts to age before it's even printed. Britain is more stable than most European countries but do what you can to double-check hours and times when you arrive.

The hours listed are for peak season. Many places close an hour earlier in off season. Some are open only on weekends or are closed entirely in the winter. Confirm your sightseeing plans locally — especially when travelling between October and May. Many sights shift into winter schedules, closing earlier, when 'British Summer Time' ends in late October.

Dave Hoerlein knows a good map is worth a thousand words. His maps make my text easy to follow. Dave points out all major landmarks, streets and accommodation mentioned in the book and he indicates the best city entry and exit routes for our itinerary. His maps are clear, concise and readable, but are designed only to orientate you and direct you until you pick up something better at the tourist information office.

To get the most our of Dave's maps, learn these symbols:

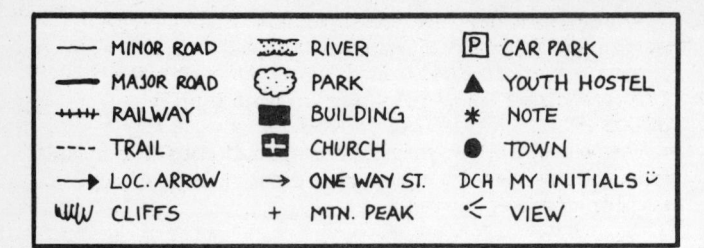

```
——  MINOR ROAD        RIVER           P  CAR PARK
——  MAJOR ROAD        PARK            ▲  YOUTH HOSTEL
++++ RAILWAY          BUILDING        *  NOTE
---- TRAIL            CHURCH          ●  TOWN
——→ LOC. ARROW    →   ONE WAY ST.    DCH MY INITIALS
WW  CLIFFS       +    MTN. PEAK         VIEW
```

Being a tourist

We travel around Great Britain to experience something different — to become temporary locals. Tourists have a knack for finding certain truths to be God-given and self evident — because they are used to having things and doing things a certain way, that to them is the 'right' way. One of the beauties of travel is the opportunity to see that there are logical, civil, and even better alternatives.

If there is a British image of tourists, especially foreign tourists, they are big, loud, a bit naive, aggressive, and rich. (Many foreign workers earn twice what their British counterparts do, and taxes, unemployment and the cost of living are all higher for the British worker).

Still, I found warmth and friendliness throughout Great Britain. An eagerness to go local and an ability — when something's not to my liking — to change my liking, made sure I enjoyed a full dose of this British hospitality.

Europeans, in general, welcome travellers and tourists if they are prepared to adapt and 'meet them half-way' — after all, we provide a source of income for many people. It is the insensitivity of some of us that the locals find objectionable. So while Europeans look bemusedly at some of our excesses — and worriedly at others — they nearly always afford individual travellers all the warmth we deserve.

Scheduling

Your overall itinerary is a fun challenge. Read through this book and note special days (festivals, colourful market days, closed days for sights etc). Sundays have pros and cons as they do for travellers everywhere (special events, limited hours, shops and banks closed, limited public transport, no rush hours). Saturdays are virtually weekdays. Popular places are even more popular on weekends — especially sunny ones, which is sufficient cause for an improptu holiday in the soggy British Isles.

It's good to alternate intense and relaxed periods. Every trip (and every traveller) needs at least a few slack days. I followed the Biblical 'one in seven' idea...religiously...on my last.

How to Use This Book

To give you a little rootedness, I've minimised one night stands. Two nights in a row, even with a hectic travel day before and after, is less gruelling than changing accommodation daily. One night stands are less of a problem when travelling off-season.

The daily suggested schedules and optional plans take many factors into account. I don't explain most of those but I hope you take the schedules seriously.

Car hire

If you plan to drive, hire a car through your travel agent well before departure. Car hire for this tour could be cheaper if booked before you leave. You'll want a weekly rate with unlimited mileage. Plan to pick up the car at Heathrow Airport on day 4 and drop it off 19 days later at Cambridge. Remember, if you drop it early or keep it longer, you'll be credited or charged at a fair, pro-rated price. Also keep in mind that you may drop the car at any location if you have a change of plans. Budget, Hertz, Avis, Kenning and Godfrey Davis all allow Heathrow pick-ups and Cambridge drops. See which is cheapest through your agent.

I normally hire the smallest, least-expensive model (eg Ford Fiesta). For a bigger, more roomy and powerful inexpensive car, move up to the Ford 1.3-litre Escort category. For peace of mind, splash out for the CDW insurance (collision damage waiver). Remember, mini-buses are a great budget way to go for 5 to 9 people.

Recommended guidebooks

This small book is only your itinerary handbook. To really enjoy and appreciate these busy weeks, you'll also need a directory-type guidebook and some good maps. I know it hurts to spend £20 or £25 ($30-$40) on extra books and maps, but when you consider the improvements they'll make in your holiday — not to mention the money they'll save you — not buying them would be perfectly 'penny-wise and pound foolish'. Here's my recommended list of supplemental information needed:

General low-budget directory-type guidebook — that is, a fatter book than this one, listing a broader range of accommodation, restaurants, sights, etc. Which one you choose depends on your budget and style of travel. My favourite by far is *Let's Go: Great Britain and Ireland*, written and thoroughly updated every year (new editions come out around March). *Let's Go* covers big cities, villages, countryside, art, entertainment, budget room and board, transport, etc. It's written for students on a student's budget and even though I'm neither, I use it every year.

Cultural and sightseeing guide — The American Express *Pocket Guide to England and Wales* and the AmExCo guide to London by Mitchell Beazley are compact and packed with handy info including a rundown on local art, history and culture, a list of all major sights, maps, and a helpful listing of hotels and restaurants for those with a little more money. The Michelin tall green guide to London is also good.

Travel philosophy — *Europe Through the Back Door* (by Rick Steves) gives you the basic skills, the foundations which make this demanding itinerary possible. Chapters on: minimising jet lag, packing light, driving vs. train travel, finding budget beds without reservations, changing money, theft and the tourist, travel photography, long distance telephoning in Europe, traveller's toilet trauma, laundry, and itinerary strategies and techniques. The book also includes special articles on 38 exciting nooks and undiscovered crannies which I call 'Back Doors'. Six are in the British Isles.

Books and maps to buy in England — Most English bookshops, especially in tourist areas, have a good selection of maps. I found a 'road Atlas' book very useful for my basic overall needs (3 miles to one inch, covering all of Britain, put out by the Ordnance Survey or by Bartholomew, about £5 ($7)). For this itinerary, I'd also pick up much more detailed maps for the Cotswold region, North Wales, Lake District, West Scotland, and North York Moors.

Foyles' Bookshop in London (near Tottenham Court Road tube stop) has the best selection of guides and maps anywhere in Britain. WH Smith shops, found in nearly every city, carry a good selection of guidebooks, maps, and local information.

As you travel you'll find racks of tempting little books at virtually every stop. The traditional finale of all British tourist attractions is a cute gift and book shoppe. Local tourist offices also abound providing lots of good printed material. Take advantage of this wealth of fascinating and helpful information. For a complete list of all you'll need that can be picked up in one stop at the London Tourist Office, see 'Tour 1'.

Freedom

This book's goal is to free you, not chain you. Please defend your spontaneity like you would your mother. Use this book to sort Britain's galaxy of sights into the most interesting, representative, diverse, and efficient programme of travel. Use it to avoid time- and money-wasting mistakes, to get more intimate with Britain by travelling without a tour — as a temporary local person. This book is a point of departure from which to shape *your* best possible travel experience. Only a real dullard would do this entire tour exactly as I've laid it out. Personalise!

Anyone who has read this far has what it takes intellectually to do this tour on their own. Be confident, militantly positive, relish the challenge and rewards of doing your own planning.

BACK DOOR TRAVEL PHILOSOPHY

AS TAUGHT IN EUROPE THROUGH THE BACK DOOR

Travel is intensified living — maximum thrills per minute and one of the last great sources of legal adventure. In many ways, the less you spend the more you get.

Experiencing the real thing requires candid informality — going 'Through the Back Door'.

Affording travel is a matter of priorities. Many people who 'can't afford a trip' could sell their car and travel for two years.

You can travel anywhere in the world for £10 (around $20) a day plus transport costs. Money has little to do with enjoying your trip. In fact, spending more money builds a thicker wall between you and what you came to see.

A tight budget forces you to travel 'close to the ground', meeting and communicating with the people, not relying on service with a purchased smile. Never sacrifice sleep, nutrition, safety or cleanliness in the name of budget. Simply enjoy the local-style alternatives to expensive hotels and restaurants.

Extroverts have more fun. If your trip is low on magic moments, kick yourself and start making things happen. Dignity and good travel don't mix.

If you don't enjoy a place it's often because you don't know enough about it. Seek out the truth. Recognise tourist traps.

A culture is legitimised by its existence. Give a people the benefit of your open mind. Think of things as different but not better or worse.

Of course, travel, like the world, is a series of hills and valleys. Be fanatically positive and militantly optimistic.

Travel is addictive. It can make you a happier person, as well as a citizen of the world. Our Earth is home to five billion equally important people. That's wonderfully humbling.

Globetrotting destroys ethno-centricity and encourages the understanding and appreciation of various cultures. Travel changes people. Many travellers toss aside their 'hometown blinkers', assimilating the best points of different cultures into their own character.

The world is a cultural garden. We're working on the ultimate salad. Won't you join us?

ITINERARY

Tour 1 Arrive in London, visit the tourist information office to lay the groundwork for the next three weeks, get set-up in your 'bed and breakfast' and take an evening walk through the heart of London.

Tour 2 Take the two-hour introductory double-decker bus tour of London before the 11:30 changing of the guard at Buckingham Palace. Then walk through the Piccadilly area to colourful Covent Garden for lunch. Spend the afternoon touring the Tower of London with a Beefeater guide and take a close look at the Crown Jewels. Then take the Thames cruise from the Bloody Tower to Westminster, landing at the foot of Big Ben. Check out Westminster Abbey, possibly visit the Houses of Parliament to see the House of Commons in action, grab some pub grub for dinner and finish the day enjoying one of London's plays.

Tour 3 London has so much to see. Spend the morning touring the British Museum. Walk down Fleet Street for a pub lunch with London's harried newspaper crowd. Climb to the summit of St. Paul's, pop in to view the action at the 'Old Bailey', the Central Criminal Court complete with powdered wigs and robes, or tour the London Stock Exchange before finishing your sightseeing day in the Museum of London.

Tour 4 Pick up your hire car at Heathrow Airport to avoid crazy London driving, and drop by Salisbury to see its cathedral. Wander through the mysterious Stonehenge and Avebury stone circles before joy-riding through several picturesque villages and into Bath.

Tour 5 Tour Bath's Roman and medieval mineral baths before a coffee break in the elegant Pump Room. Follow a local guide for two hours of history and highlights of England's trend-setting old world Hollywood. Spend the afternoon browsing and touring England's greatest collection of costumes — three hundred years of fashion history.

Tour 6 Today, sidetrip south exploring the haunted and entertaining Wookey Hole Caves, Wells with its medieval centre and striking cathedral, and mystical Glastonbury — mythical home of Avalon, King Arthur and the Holy Grail. Evening free in Bath.

Tour 7 We'll drive into Wales, through its capital of Cardiff and to St. Fagan's Folk Museum — a park full of Welsh culture,

Tour Route

HIGHLANDS
INVERNESS
LOCH NESS
-16-
SCOTLAND
BEN NEVIS
PITLOCHRY
0 40 80
MILES
OBAN -15-
EDINBURGH -17, 18-
GLASGOW
HADRIAN'S WALL
N. IRE.
-19-
DURHAM
BELFAST
LAKE DIST. -13, 14-
NORTH YORK MOORS -20-
YORK -21-
BLACKPOOL -12-
ENGLAND
DUBLIN
LIVERPOOL
IRELAND
-11-
RUTHIN
CAERNARFON
IRONBRIDGE GORGE
SNOWDONIA
-10-
COVENTRY
-9-
WARWICK
ROSSLARE
WALES
STRATFORD
COTSWOLD
CAMBRIDGE -22-
TINTERN
STOW -8-
-7-
CARDIFF
BATH -5-
LONDON -1,2,3-
WELLS
-4-
-6-
SALISBURY
GLASTONBURY
STONEHENGE
OVERNIGHTS
DAY VISITS
DCH

Itinerary 17

restored old houses, and an intimate look at this fascinating culture. After a scenic drive up the Wye River valley, past Tintern Abbey and through the Forest of Dean, we'll set up at Stow-on-the-Wold in the heart of the Cotswold hills.

Tour 8 Spend half the day savouring the most delicious of England's villages, the quintessence of quaint. Then visit Blenheim Palace.

Tour 9 After a morning in Shakespeare's hometown, Stratford, we'll tour England's finest medieval castle at Warwick and see the inspirational Coventry Cathedral — a charred ruin from the 'blitz' with a shiny new church built more with love than with nails.

Tour 10 Today is devoted to the birthplace of the Industrial Revolution. The Ironbridge Gorge on the Severn River is a series of museums that take the visitor back into those heady days when Britain was racing into the modern age and pulling the rest of the West with her. Then it's into the romantic beauty of North Wales, setting up in Ruthin.

Tour 11 Circling scenic and historic North Wales, we'll tour a woollen mill, the Caernarfon Castle, awesome Mount Snowdon and a bleak slate mine, arriving home in time to indulge in a medieval Welsh banquet — complete with harp, singing, mead and daggers for meat-eating.

Tour 12 From the Garden of Eden to the garden of Hedon-ism, we'll drive to Blackpool for a look at the most popular tourist attraction in Britain ... that all visitors skip. Six miles of fortune tellers, fish 'n chips, amusement piers, beaches, warped mirrors and hordes of English. It's playtime!

Tour 13 For another splash of contrast, we'll drive into the pristine Lake District, inspiration for Wordsworth, with enough natural beauty to make anyone a poet. After a short cruise, and a six-mile walk around the lovliest of these lovely lakes, we'll check into a remote farmhouse B&B.

Tour 14 A pilgrimage to Wordsworth's famous Dove Cottage is in order before enjoying a free day to relax, recharge, and take the walk of your choice.

Tour 15 Now north into Scotland, past bustling Glasgow, along the scenic Loch Lomond for a six hour drive to the Highlands. Blaring bagpipes and swirling kilts accompany dinner tonight.

Tour 16 Today's all-day joy-ride features the stark beauty of Glencoe, scene of a bloody clan massacre, a drive from coast to coast along the Caledonian Canal and Loch Ness. Even if you don't see the monster, you will tour a grand castle and enjoy some fine Highland scenery. After a visit to Culloden, the site of the last battle on British soil — and the end of Bonnie Prince Charlie and Scottish hopes, you'll zip down from Inverness to Edinburgh.

Tour 17 Edinburgh! one of Europe's most entertaining cities. After a tourist office orientation, we'll cover the Royal Mile, touring the Edinburgh Castle, Holyrood Palace — where the Queen stays when she's in town — and everything in between. This is the colourful city of Robert Louis Stevenson, Walter Scott and Robert Burns.

Tour 18 There's much more to see and do in Edinburgh: a concert in the park, the elegantly Georgian new town, the best shopping in Scotland, and an evening of folk music and dance.

Tour 19 Two hours south of Edinburgh, Hadrian's Wall reminds us that Britain was an important Roman colony two thousand years ago. After a walk along Hadrian's ramparts and through a fine Roman museum, it's on to the fascinating Beamish Open Air Museum for a look at life in the dawn of our century. Finally, we'll tour Durham Cathedral, England's finest Norman church.

Tour 20 After a morning on the lonesome North York Moors with its time-passed villages, bored sheep and powerful landscapes, we'll set up in the city of York in time to enjoy an introductory walking tour by an old Yorker.

Tour 21 York has more than its share of block-buster sights. We'll divide this day between the great York Minster, the Jorvik exhibit — the best Viking museum anywhere — and several engrossing hours in the York Castle Museum — a walk with Charles Dickens.

Tour 22 After a three-hour drive to Cambridge, we'll leave our bags at the station, turn our car in, and spend the afternoon exploring England's lovliest cluster of colleges. Cambridge, with its sleepy river, lush green grounds, mellow study halls, helpful tourist office and old streets clogged with bicycles, is worth all the time you can muster today before catching the hour long train ride into London. The circle is complete and you've experienced the best 22 days Britain has to offer. Of course, next year you may want 22 more.

Itinerary

On this trip you'll see:
City tours: London, Bath, Edinburgh, York, and Cambridge.
Churches: Salisbury (spire — Gothic), Wells (arch and carving — Gothic), Coventry (WW II reconcilliation and modern art), Durham (best Norman or Romanesque), York Minster (windows and undercroft — Gothic), Cambridge — King's College (windows and fan vaulting — high Gothic), and St. Paul's (London view — Wren architecture).
Castles: Tower of London, Warwick, Caernarfon and Edinburgh.
Ancient sites: Stonehenge, Avebury, Bath — Roman Spa, Hadrian's Wall and Fort.
Palaces: Blenheim, and Holyrood.
Abbeys: Glastonbury, and Tintern.
Historical museums: Museum of London, British Museum (London), Fitzwilliam Museum (Cambridge), Jorvik Viking Exhibit (York), Costume Museum (Bath), Georgian house (Bath), Wordsworth's Dove Cottage, and several small houses of history along Edinburgh's Royal Mile.
Art museums: National Gallery (London), Tate Gallery (London), and Fitzwilliam (Cambridge).
Folk museums: St. Fagan's (Cardiff — Welsh), Ironbridge Gorge (Industrial Revolution), Beamish (Life in 1900), and York Castle Museum (Life 1700-1900).
Great landscape: Cotswold hills and villages, North Wales — Snowdonia National Park, Cumbria — Lake District, Scottish Highlands, and North York Moors.
Miscellaneous fun and culture: London Theatre, Wookey Hole Caves, Medieval Welsh Banquet, Slate Mine Tour, Evensong Service, and Blackpool Amusements.

TOUR 1
FLY TO LONDON

On this busy first day you'll leave your familiar world, set up and settle in for a night in one of the world's most exciting cities—London.

Suggested Schedule

Arrive at London Airport if flying, travel into town. Follow 'Arrival in London' instructions carefully.

Check into hotel, hostel or bed and breakfast.

Visit tourist info at Victoria Station (possibly en route to hotel) for London and Britain information and play tickets. Make trip-organising phone calls from hotel.

Bus to Westminster Bridge for your 'first night walk'.

(Note: If your plane arrives in the morning, you may have time to take the Round London orientation this afternoon, freeing some time tomorrow.)

Flying

Call the airport before leaving home to be sure your plane's on schedule. Combat boredom and frustration from the inevitable delays and queues by bringing something to do — book, journal, some handwork. Expect delays and remember no matter how long it takes, flying is a very easy, spaceage way to get there. If you haven't already read this book carefully from cover to cover, do so, making notes during the flight.

To minimise jet lag (body clock adjustment, stress if flying long distance:

★ Leave well rested. Schedule a false departure day one day early. Plan accordingly, and, even at the cost of hecticity the day before, enjoy a peaceful last day.

★ During the flight, minimise stress by eating lightly, avoiding alcohol, caffeine and sugar. Drink juice.

★ Sleep through the in-flight film — or at least close your eyes and pretend (unless you're reading *Great Britain in Your Pocket*).

★ Change your watch to London time.

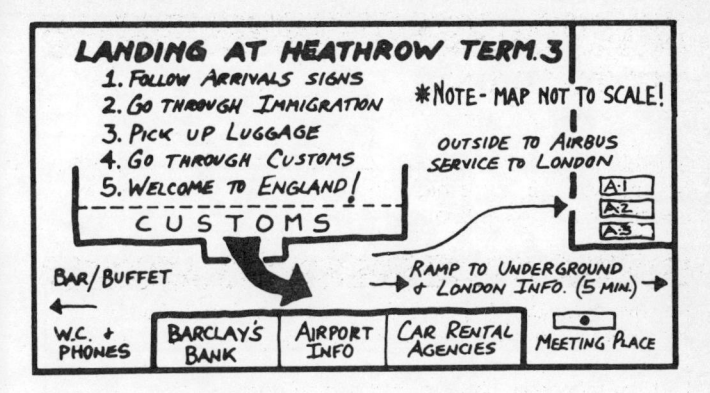

Arrival in London

This section assumes that you are flying to London. From the aircraft, follow the 'arrivals' signs to baggage and customs. Heathrow Airport has a reputation for being confusing. Ask questions. (The locals speak English.) Collect your baggage and proceed to customs. The customs official will take a quick look at your passport, ask you a few questions to be sure you're adequately financed and not a spy, and wave you through. After customs you'll pop into throngs of waiting loved-ones. You'll see a Barclays Bank (open 24-hours daily) and an Information desk. Change plenty of money, and buy a £5 bag of 10p coins for phone calls and future parking. At the terminal info desk, pick up a London map, ask about transport into London by Airbus or tube and get directions to the Heathrow tourist information office. You might also drop by your car hire agency's desk to confirm your pick-up plans on day 4. Then follow the signs to the underground (a long walk on a moving ramp) to the T.1. This airport tourist office (open 9:00-6:00 daily) is less crowded than the Victoria Station office in town. Get whatever info you'd like and consider buying your 'Explorer ticket' (to cover your trip into London), and your 'Open to View' ticket. The T.I. is at the tube stop, or you can walk back into the airport to catch the Airbus.

Transport into London

The fastest and easiest cheap way into London is by tube or Airbus — depending on where your hotel is. Buses leave Heathrow constantly: A1 to Victoria Station, A2 to Paddington Station and A3 to Euston Station with stops along the way — around £3 ($5). Most of my hotel recommendations are on the A2 Airbus line near Notting Hill Gate (the stop after the Hilton Hotel).

To save money, buy an Explorer transit ticket at the tube ticket window and use it on this bus ride. This gives you

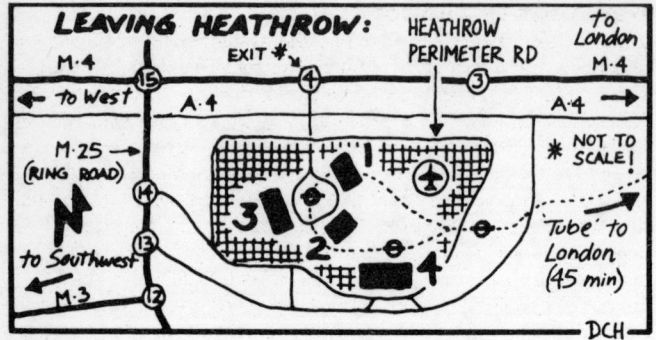

```
LEAVING HEATHROW:    HEATHROW         to
  M·4         EXIT #   PERIMETER RD   London
                                      M·4
← to West    A·4                      A·4 →
                                      * NOT TO
  M·25 →                                SCALE!
  (RING ROAD)
                                      Tube to
to Southwest                          London
                                      (45 min)
  M·3
                                      DCH
```

unlimited bus and tube travel throughout London, including Airbus and tube to and from Heathrow. While the tube works fine, I prefer taking the Airbus into London — there are no connections underground and a lovely view from the top of the double-decker. The driver will remind you when to get off if you ask him to.

Most flights arrive at Heathrow but some charters go into Gatwick Airport. Trains shuttle between Gatwick and Victoria Station four times an hours (a 30-minute ride).

Orientation

London, over 600 square miles of urban jungle with seven million struggling people, is a world in itself, a barrage on all the senses, and a place that can make you feel very small. It's much more than museums and famous landmarks. It's a living, breathing organism that somehow manages to thrive.

London has changed dramatically in recent years and many visitors are surprised to find how 'un-English' it is. Whites are actually a minority now in a city that once symbolised white imperialism. Arabs have pretty much bought out the area north of Hyde Park. Fish and chips shops are now out-numbered by Chinese take-aways (or 'fee n' chee shops' as locals call them). Most hotels are run or at least staffed by people with foreign accents, while outlying suburbs are huge communities of blacks, Pakistanis, Indians and Asians. London is learning — sometimes fitfully — to live as a microcosm of its formerly vast empire.

With just three nights and two days here we'll get no more than a quick splash in this teeming human tidepool. But hopefully, with some quick orientation, we'll get a good sampling of its top sights, history, cultural entertainment and ever-changing human face.

London has all the pitfalls of any big city, but if you're on the ball, informed and well-organised it won't cost a fortune, you won't get ripped-off, and you'll leave ready for the more peaceful countryside but looking forward to your return.

Transport in London

London's taxis, buses and underground system make a private car unnecessary. In a city this size, you must get comfortable with its public transport. Don't be timid; dive in, take the bull by the horns, and in no time you'll have London by the tail.

Taxis — Big, black, carefully regulated cabs are everywhere. I never met a crabby cabbie in London. They love to talk and know every nook and cranny in town. Journeys start at 80p and stay surprisingly reasonable. There are often extra charges (legitimate ones) added on, but usually two or three people in a cab travel at tube prices. If the top light is on just wave one down. Telephoning is unnecessary — taxis are everywhere.

Buses — London's extensive bus system is easy to follow if you have a map listing the routes (as on most tourist maps). Signs at the stops list exactly where the buses go, and conductors are terse but helpful. Ask to be reminded when it's your stop. Just hop on and take a seat (I always go upstairs for the best view). You'll be ticketed whenever the conductor gets around to it. Buses and taxis are miserable during rush hours — 8-10 am and 4-7 pm. Journeys vary from 30p to over a pound.

Underground — The London 'tube' is one of this planet's great people movers. Every city map includes a tube map. You'll need it. Navigate by colour-coded lines and north (always up on the map), south, east or west. You buy your ticket before descending — at the window or from coin-op machines to avoid the queue — then hang onto it, giving it to a collector as you leave the system. Read system notices and signs carefully, ask questions of locals, and watch your wallet. You'll find that 'tubing' is by far the fastest long-distance transport in town. It used to be fiercely expensive but now is a reasonable 30p to £1.50 per journey.

Special money-saving transit tickets

Nearly every tourist should take advantage of one of these underground/bus 'go as you please' specials. Available on the spot in tube stations, they give you unlimited travel on all buses and tubes.

Explorer Pass — 1 day — £3 ($5), 3 days — £9 ($15), 4 days — £11 ($20) and 7 days — £14 ($25), covering the entire system including tube and Airbus to and from Heathrow airport.

Travelcard — 7 days unlimited coverage within the underground 'Circle' line for £4 ($7). Few tourists take advantage of this, though nearly every major tourist sight is covered in this central circle. The airport trip, unfortunately, isn't covered. Pick this card up in any tube station (photo required). Travelcards are available covering even bigger areas and longer durations.

Cheap day returns — The English love to encourage round trips on train, tube or bus with R/T fares often just barely more than one-way.

Ask at any tube station for a brochure about special passes. It makes no sense to pre-purchase any these abroad. But wise travellers pick them up upon arrival to cover the journey in from Heathrow.

London information

You can't do London without information. Good guidebooks abound. (I like *Let's Go Britain* and London guides by Michelin, Mitchell Beazley, and Frommer. The new *Virgin Guide to London* is a refreshingly opinionated guide for 'hip' travellers.) The free London transport and tourist map (available at the Tourist Information office, some tube stations and hotels) is good enough, but the first class map is ideal.

Tourist offices are located at Heathrow airport, in Victoria Station (tel. 730-3488, open daily 9:00-8:30, 8:00-10:00 in July and August), at Selfridges in Oxford Street and at Harrods (regular shop hours). The Victoria Station office has a great selection of books covering all of Britain, a room-finding service (not cheap), and a helpful staff with a huge arsenal of leaflets, lists, maps and printed advice. They can also sell you theatre tickets.

For the best listing of what's going on this week (plays, films, restaurants, concerts, exhibitions, walking tours, protests, what to do with children, etc) pick up a current copy of 'What's On' at any newsstand. ('Time Out' and 'City Limits' are hip and more opinionated versions of 'Whats On'. You can also telephone 246-8041 for a taped listing of today's happenings. For 'Children's London' dial 246-8807.)

At the tourist info desk, have a check list. Go over your London plans, buy a ticket to a play, and pick up these publications:
  Events and Entertainment, theatre guide
  Directory of Tourist Info Centres
  'What's On' (or 'Time Out' or 'City Limits')
  Quick Guide to London — 50p.
Then go around the corner to the National Tourist Centre bookshop.

National tourist information

The energetic British Tourist Authority has opened an impressive new national tourist info centre just off Piccadilly Circus (12 Regent Street, tel. 730-3400, open Monday-Saturday 9-6:30, Sunday 10-4). In this huge centre you'll find an extensive travel bookshop, an expensive (£4 ($7) charge) room-finding service for the entire British Isles (including London), a British Rail Info desk, an American Express Bank as well as the helpful tourist info desk. This is the place to gather whatever info, maps, etc you'll need during your entire trip so you'll pull into each stop on this itinerary well prepared. I'd recommend the following books and maps (approximate prices):

★ A Road Atlas (the AA edition) £3.75 ($7)
★ Let's Go: Britain (if you don't already have it) £7 ($12)
★ Youth Hostel Association 1988 guide (if you plan to) £1.25 ($2)
★ American Express Guides to London and England (each by Mitchell Beazley) £4.95 ($9)
★ Stonehenge and Avebury (picture book) £1.25 ($2)
★ Wales Tourist Map — 95p ($1.50)
★ Tourist Guide to North Wales £1.20 ($2)
★ Tourist Guide to South Wales £1.20 ($2)
★ Cotswolds Wyedean Official Tourist Map (covering Tintern to Coventry) £1.95 ($3)
★ Shropshire (Heart of England Tourist Board) 95p ($1.50)
★ Lake District Tourist Map (Ordnance Survey) £2.40 ($4)
★ The Good Guide to the Lakes (Hunter Davies) £2.95 ($5)
★ Leisure Map Touring Scotland £1.50 ($3)
(And consider the many enticing guides and maps to London)

That's around £35 ($55), but it's worth it to be really prepared to travel smart. You are your own guide — be a good one.

Within a block of the British National Tourist Centre you'll find the Scottish Tourist Centre (19 Cockspur Street, tel. 930-8661) and the Welsh Tourist Centre (34 Piccadilly, tel. 409-0969).

Accommodation

Cheap, central and comfortable — pick two. With London's great underground, I'll sacrifice centrality for a cheery place that won't ruin my budget. London has hundreds of hotels but few great deals. There's no need, however, to spend a fortune or stay in a dangerous, depressing dump.

Reserve your London room in advance with a phone call direct from home. Assure them that you'll arrive before 4:00 pm, or send a signed travellers cheque covering at least the first night. (Include a note explaining that you'll be happy to pay cash upon arrival so they can avoid bank charges if they'll just hold your cheque until you get there.)

Here are a few of my favourites:

Hotel Ravna Gora — Located just across from the Holland Park tube station. Formerly Mr. Holland's mansion, now it's a large B&B run by supporters of the long-exiled King of Yugoslavia. A bit eccentric and well worn — still, you won't find a more comfortable or handy place for the price. Manda and Rijko take good care of their guests while downstairs the Serbian royalists quaff beer and dream of a glorious restoration some day. Royal TV room, good English breakfast, on the Central tube line, Airbus A2 uphill from Kensington Hilton.

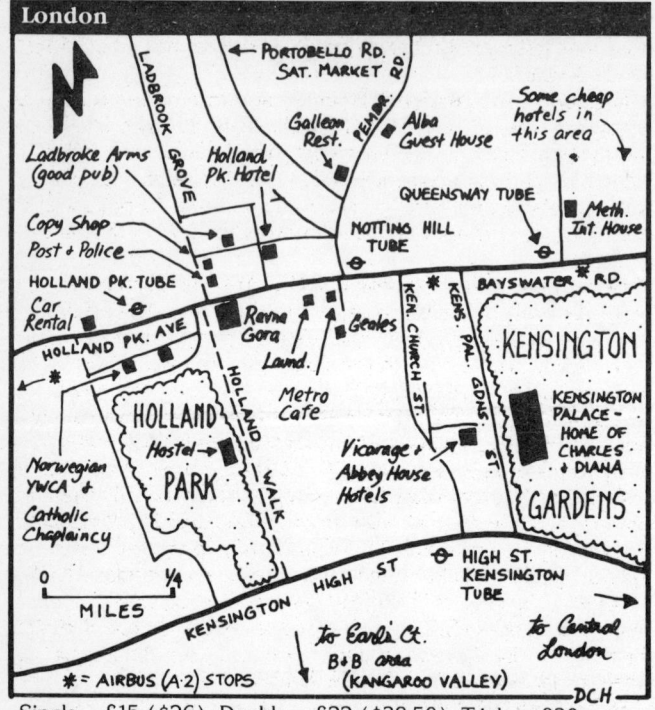

[Map of London showing Holland Park, Kensington area with hotels and landmarks labeled: Portobello Rd. Sat. Market, Ladbrook Grove, Galleon Rest., Alba Guest House, "Some cheap hotels in this area", Ladbroke Arms (good pub), Holland Pk. Hotel, Pembr. Rd., Queensway Tube, Copy Shop, Post & Police, Notting Hill Tube, Meth. Int. House, Holland Pk. Tube, Car Rental, Ravna Gora, Geales, Bayswater Rd., Holland Pk. Ave., Ken. Church St., Kens. Pal. Gdns., Kensington Palace - Home of Charles & Diana, Laund., Metro Cafe, Holland Park, Hostel, Vicarage & Abbey House Hotels, Holland Walk, Norwegian YWCA & Catholic Chaplaincy, Kensington Gardens, High St. Kensington Tube, Kensington High St., to Earl's Ct. B+B area (Kangaroo Valley), to Central London, * = AIRBUS (A·2) STOPS, 0 - 1/4 MILES, DCH]

Single — £15 ($26), Double — £22 ($38.50), Triple — £30 ($52.50), Quads — £40 ($70). At 29 Holland Park Avenue, London W11, tel. 727-7725.

Vicarage Private Hotel, 10, Vicarage Gate, Kensington, London W8, tel. 229-4030, is very popular, family-run in a quiet, classy neighbourhood midway between Notting Hill Gate and High Street Kensington tube stations near Kensington Palace. Smaller, cosier and more expensive than Ravna Gora. Prices with English breakfast and shower down the hall are: Single — £15 ($26), Double — £26 ($45), Triple — £33 ($58), Quad — £37 ($65). Make reservations long in advance with phone call followed by one night's deposit (travellers cheques in pounds).

Abbey House Hotel, 11 Vicarage Gate, Kensington, London, W8, tel. 727-2594, is similar in almost every way to its neighbour the Vicarage Private Hotel. A few pounds more expensive. Friendly management. One night deposit required (£30 ($50) signed travellers cheque is fine).

Alba Guest House, 53 Pembridge Villas, London W11, tel. 727-8910 is very small, friendly and family run in a funky but pleasant locale at the foot of colourful Portobello Road, a block from the Notting Hill tube station. Run by Raymond Khoo, £26 ($45) doubles.

Methodist International House — at 4 Inverness Terrace near Bayswater tube, tel. 229-5101. This Christian residence filled mostly with Third World students is great if you want a truly world-wide dormitory experience. £12 ($20) for a shared room with breakfast and a great dinner. Don't miss the 10 pm social hour with tea and biscuits. Open to travellers only in July and August.

Norwegian YWCA (Norsk K.F.U.K.) — For women only (and men with Norwegian passports), this is incredible value — lovely atmosphere, on quiet stately street, piano lounge, TV room, study, all rooms with private shower, all three meals included, single — £12.50 ($22), double — £10.50 ($18), triple £9.50 ($16), and £8.50 ($15) each in quads. They have mostly quads so if you're willing to share with strangers you're most likely to get a place. Tel. 727-9897, 52 Holland Park, W11 3R5.

Catholic International Chaplaincy — Another gem, open to both men and women but only from mid-June to September 30, Father Maguire provides a TV lounge, study room, self-service kitchen, garden, breakfast and a very pleasant atmosphere for £8 ($14) in a single or only £6 ($10) in a double or triple. He will make reservations (£12 or $20 signed traveller's cheque deposit) for those staying for a week. Otherwise, call from the airport when you land. Tel. 727-3047, 41 Holland Park, W11 3RP.

Dean Court Hotel — Wild, crazy, full of Aussies, charges £7-10 ($12-18) per night, at 57 Inverness Terrace, tel. 229-2961.

Coleman Lodge Hotel — Big, hip, scruffy but comfortable, this is the best cheap hotel I've found in the centre. Student-orientated, bar, laundry, TV lounge, £9 ($16) per person in double room with English breakfast. 31 Craven Hill Gardens, W2, tel. 723-5988, near Lancaster Gate and Bayswater tube stations.

Youth Hostels — London has five or six official and more unofficial hostels. Personally, I'd stick to the official ones, but all are the large, impersonal, regimented big-city variety. They are very popular, always fill up, are equipped with good facilities, and are the cheapest beds in town — around £4 ($7).

Harlingford Hotel at 61 Cartwright Gardens, tel. 387-1551, is very well run and comfortable. Located near the British Museum (Russell Square tube) on a crescent with several other good budget B&Bs, £28 ($50) doubles.

Holland Park Hotel — The most 'hotellesque' of any of these places. Still, Roy and Jean Allen run this good value with a personal touch. £20 ($35) single, £27 ($48) double, £45 ($78) triple, £55 ($96) quad (more with private showers), TVs in each room, English breakfast, quiet, pleasant street, will accept telephone reservations without deposits if you'll arrive by mid-afternoon. 6 Ladbrook Terrace, W11 3PG, tel. 727-8166.

Near Victoria Station — Belgrave Road, Warwick Way and St. George Way are lined with reasonable B&B's.

Food

London has plenty of fine restaurants — charging very high prices. If you want to dine (as opposed to eat), check out the extensive listings in 'What's On'. The American Express London guidebook is a reliable source with more opinions. The thought of a £15 ($25) meal generally ruins my appetite so my dining here is mostly limited to unremarkable but wonderfully inexpensive alternatives.

Pub grub is your most atmospheric option. Many of London's 7,000 pubs (I counted them myself one night) serve fresh and tasty buffets under ancient timbers with hearty lunches and dinner costing £3-4 ($5-7). Ethnic restaurants from all over the world more than make up for the basically lacklustre English cuisine. Eating Indian or Chinese is 'going local' in London. It's also going cheap.

Fish 'n chips are still popular and easy to find. The best fish 'n chips in town in a comfy setting near my recommended B&Bs is the very popular **Geale's** at 2 Farmer Street, just off Notting Hill Gate. Open Tuesday-Saturday, 12-3 and 6-11. Get there early for the best selections.

And of course the picnic is the fastest, healthiest and cheapest way to go. There are plenty of good food shops and fine park benches in Britain's most expensive city.

First night walk

Now that you're set up for the night in London, it's time to enjoy a very relaxed introduction to the city. This walk is a pleasant orientation, and also a great way to stay awake on the evening of your arrival.

Catch a bus down to Westminster Bridge (No. 12 or 88 from Notting Hill Gate, sit on the top deck). Walk halfway across the bridge to view the floodlit Houses of Parliament and Big Ben to get that 'Wow, I'm really in London!' feeling. Grab a light dinner at Grandma Lee's Restaurant across from Big Ben next to the tube station.

Then cross Whitehall, noticing the Churchill Statue in the park. (He's electrified to avoid the pigeon problem that stains so many other great statues.) Walk up towards Trafalgar Square. Stop at the barricaded and guarded little Downing Street to see No. 10, home of the British Prime Minister. Break the bobbie's boredom — ask him a question. Just before Trafalgar Square, drop into the Clarence Pub for a pint of whatever you fancy.

From Trafalgar Square walk to thriving Leicester Square and continue to Piccadilly.

For seediness, walk through Soho (north of Shaftesbury Avenue) up to Oxford Street. From Piccadilly or Oxford Circus you can taxi, bus or tube home. Why not teach yourself the underground system now? With all this activity, you're more likely to get some good sleep on the traditionally fitful first night.

TOUR 2
AROUND LONDON

The sights of London alone could easily fill a book like this. Today and tomorrow will be spent enjoying as many of these sights as time and energy will allow. Obviously, this is only a suggested itinerary. You'll have two days in which to pick and choose among all the things listed here.

Suggested Schedule

8:00 am	Breakfast, tube or bus to Marble Arch.
9:00 am	Catch Round London Tour.
11:00 am	Taxi to Buckingham Palace for 11:30 Changing of the Guard. Or practise a little urban immersion — strolling, window-shopping and people watching your way from Marble Arch along Oxford Street, Regent Street, Soho, Piccadilly and Leicester Square to Covent Garden.
1:00 pm	Lunch in Covent Garden — no shortage of intriguing food and colourful surroundings.
2:00 pm	Walk the Strand to the Temple tube station and underground to Tower Hill. Tour the Tower of London starting with the Beefeater Tour. Don't miss the Crown Jewels.
5:00 pm	Sail from the Tower to Westminster Bridge enjoying a thirty-minute commentary on the Thames. Westminster Abbey is open until 6:00 and the Visitors Gallery in the Houses of Parliament is open, when in session, from 6:00. (If you have a play to see or are travelling in summer, this schedule is probably too much unless you're really speedy.)
7:00 pm	Pub dinner near your theatre.
8:00 pm	Most plays start at 8:00 pm; enjoy the one of your choice.

Sightseeing highlights

After considering nearly all of London's tourist sights, I have painfully pruned them down to just the most important (or fun) for a first visit. You won't be able to see even all of these - so don't try. You'll keep coming back to London. After 15 visits myself, I still enjoy a healthy list of excuses to return.

● ● **Round London Tour** - This orientation tour is your best intro. London Transport gives these 90-minute 'stay on the bus

Tour 2

and enjoy a light once over of all the famous sights with a great commentary' double-decker tours for £5 ($8). Tours leave daily on the half-hour from 9:00 to 4:00 plus 6:00 from Marble Arch, Piccadilly Circus and Victoria Station (Grosvenor Gardens). No reservations necessary.

● **Walking tours** - Every day several walking tours explore specific slices of London's past. These are listed in 'What's On', and the Tourist Info has plenty of leaflets. You just show up at the announced location, pay £2 or so ($3.50), and enjoy two hours of Dickens, the Plague, Shakespeare, Jack the Ripper, or whatever is on the menu. Evenings feature organised pub crawls and 'ghost walks'.

● ● ● **Tower of London** - Don't miss the entertaining Beefeater tour (free, leaving regularly from inside the gate). Best armoury in Britain is in the White Tower. Get your armour education in here. Lovely Norman chapel. Crown Jewels are the best on earth - and consequently have 2-hour queues mid-day in July and August. To avoid the crowds, arrive at 9:30 and go straight to the jewels, doing the Tower later. (Tower hours: Open Mon-Sat 9:30-5:45, Sun 2:00-5:45. The long queue moves fast usually, but is slowest on Sundays.)

Great tourist office across from the Tower entrance. St. Katherine Yacht Harbour, chic and newly renovated, just past the freshly painted Tower Bridge with historic boats and mod shops. Classic old pub, the Dickens Inn, fun for a drink or lunch. Boat tours with a very good commentary sail regularly between Westminster Bridge and the Tower (30 minutes around £1 ($2)). Best bit of London's Roman Wall just north of tower. (Tube: Tower Hill).

● ● ● **Westminster** - The Abbey, Houses of Parliament and Whitehall.

Westminster Abbey is a crowded collection of England's most famous tombs. Historic, thought-provoking, but a bit over-rated, open 8:00-6:00, till 8:00 on Wednesdays.

The Houses of Parliament are too tempting to terrorists to be open to tourists. But you can view the House of Commons when it's sitting, Monday-Thursday 2;30-10:00 pm - long waits until 6:00, use St. Stephens entrance - no bags allowed, phone 219-4272 for details. Don't miss the view from the bridge. You won't actually see Big Ben, the 13-ton bell (with the famous 'dong dong dong dong dong dong dong dong' tune) inside the neo-Gothic tower; you'll hear him, though. Remember, these old-looking buildings are Neo-Gothic - just 100 years old, reflecting the Victorian move away from Neo-classicism and into a more 'Christian', medieval style.

Whitehall, the centre of government boulevard, runs from Big Ben to Trafalgar Square, past lots of important but boring

buildings. Stop by No. 10 Downing Street, the Royal Horse
Guard's (10:00-4:00, 11:00 inspection, 4:00 colourful
dismounting ceremony, the rest of the day - very still, lots of
photos), the Banqueting Hall (England's first Renaissance
building by Inigo Jones in 1625), and the atmospheric Clarence
Pub. The newly opened Cabinet War Rooms, Churchill's
underground headquarters during the 'Blitz', are fascinating. Only
a 3-minute walk from Big Ben. For the best view, cross the
bridge, go along the promenade to the left at dusk.

● ● **Trafalgar Square** - London's central square, and a thrilling
place just to hang out. There's Lord Nelson's towering column
surrounded by giant lions made from the melted-down cannons
of his victims at Trafalgar, hordes of people and even more
pigeons. The square is the climax of most marches and
demonstrations. Nearby is The National Gallery with paintings by
Leonardo, Caravaggio, Velazquez, the Impressionists, and Jan Van
Eyck's great Arnolfini Marriage (free, Monday-Saturday
10:00-6:00, Sunday 2:00-6:00) and the less exciting National
Portrait Gallery.

● ● **Piccadilly** - The 'hub' of London is surrounded by fascinating
streets and neighbourhoods. Shaftesbury Avenue and Leicester
Square teem with fun-seekers, theatres, Chinese restaurants and
street singers. Soho, to the north, seethes with sleazier activities

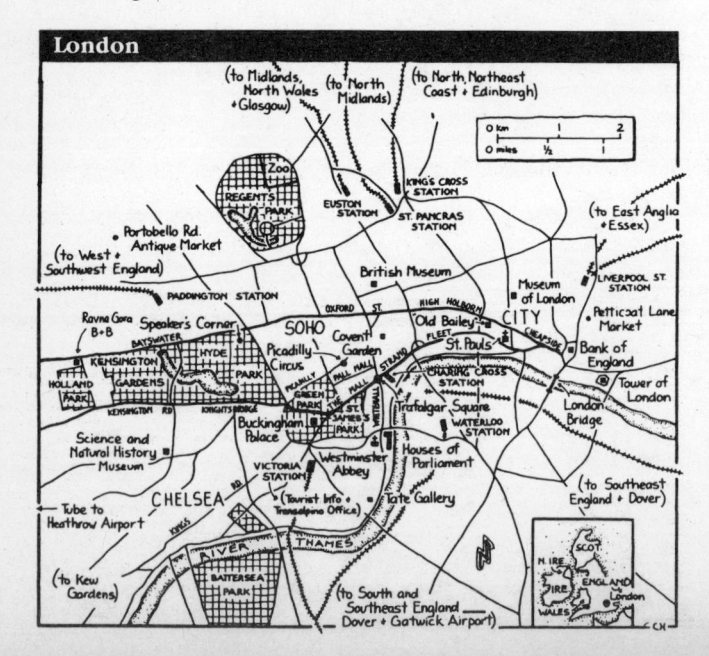

and is worth at least a glimpse. Walk up Berwick Street to Oxford Street and check out the formerly trendy, now tacky Carnaby Street. The shiny new Trocadero Centre has the Guiness World Records Exhibit and the touristy but fun London Experience film (10:20 am — 10:20 pm daily, around £2 ($3.50)). The whole area between Regent Street, Oxford Street, Kingsway and the Strand is titillating to say the least. Covent Garden is especially fun with its buskers, antique shops, liberal bookshops, far-out crowds and imaginative eateries.

- **Buckingham Palace** and **Changing of the Guard** — Overrated but almost required. You'll only see the back side of the palace, as the front faces a huge and very private park. The royal residence of London is never open to the public (although if you look sincere and ask the guard if you can sign the visitor's book, he may escort you in). The changing of the guard, almost daily in summer at 11:30, every other day in winter, is a mob scene. The best view is from the top of the Victoria Monument. The pageantry and parading are colourful and even stirring, but the actual changing of the guard is a non-event. Hop in a big black taxi and say 'to Buckingham Palace, please'. Stroll through St. James Park nearby.
- **Hyde Park** - London's central park with over 600 acres of lush greenery, a huge man-made lake, a royal palace (Kensington, worth touring) and the ornate Neo-Gothic Albert memorial across from the Royal Albert Hall. On Sunday afternoons, check out Speaker's Corner, at Marble Arch. This is soap-box oratory at its best, the grassroots of democracy.
- **Harrods** - One of the few stores in the world to combine size and class. Wonderful displays, elegant high teas, thrilling riots during the July sales. Harrods has everything from elephants to toothbrushes.

Street markets - If you like garage sales and people-watching, try to hit a London street market. The tourist office has a complete list. A few of the best are: Berwick Street (tube: Piccadilly Circus, Monday-Saturday, produce), Jubilee Market (tube: Covent Garden, 9:00-4:00, antiques and bric-a-brac on Mondays, general miscellaneous on Tuesday-Friday, crafts on Saturday and Sunday), Kensington Market (tube: High Street Kensington, Monday-Saturday 10:00-6:00, modern and far-out clothing), Petticoat Lane (Middlesex Street, tube: Liverpool Street, Sunday, 9:00-1:30, general junk), Portobello Road (near recommended B&Bs, tube: Notting Hill Gate; Monday-Friday general, Saturday flea market, 9:00-5:00), and Camden Lock (the biggest flea market on Saturdays and Sundays, 9:00-6:00, tube Camden Town). Warning: street markets attract two kinds of people - tourists and pickpockets.

● ● ● **British Museum** - The greatest chronicle of our civilisation anywhere, this immense museum can only be dipped into. Take a long walk - like hiking through Encyclopaedia Britannica National Park — then cover just two or three sections of your choice more thoroughly. The Egyptian, Mesopotamian, Greek (Parthenon) and Manuscripts (Magna Carta) sections are a few of my favourites. Free, open Monday-Saturday 10:00-5:00, Sunday 2:30-6:00 (tube: Tottenham Court Road).

● ● **Tate Gallery** - One of Europe's great houses of art, the Tate specialises in British painting (1500 - contemporary, with great Turner and Blake collections) and in international modern art (Matisse, Van Gogh, Monet). Learn about the mystical watercolourist Blake and the Romantic nature-worship art of Turner. Lots of tours, a great gift shop. Free, open Monday-Saturday 10:00 - 6:00, Sunday 2:00-6:00 (tube: Pimlico).

● ● **The City of London** - When Londoners say 'the City', they mean the one-square-mile business, banking and journalism centre that 2,000 years ago was Roman Londinium. The outline of the Roman City Walls can still be seen in the arc of roads from Blackfriars Bridge to the Tower Bridge. Within the city are 24 churches designed by Christopher Wren.

Wren's most famous church is the great St. Paul's, with an elaborate interior capped by a 365-foot dome. St. Paul's is the symbol of British resistance, as Nazi bombs actually bounced off it in World War II. It was the wedding church of Prince Charles and Lady Di. Climb the dome for a great city view and some fun in the whispering gallery - talk into the wall and your partner on the far side can hear you. (Tours 11:00, 11:30, 2:00, 2:30, open 8:00-6:00. Allow an hour to go up and down the dome - it's good exercise).

A place near and dear to the busy people in three-piece suits and 'tightly-wrapped' umbrellas that clog that city by day is The Stock Exchange (free tours Monday-Fridays, 9:45-3:30). Also worth a look is the Central Criminal Court known as the 'Old Bailey'. An hour in the visitors' gallery (Monday-Friday 10:15-1:00, 2:00-4:00, closed in August) is always fascinating.

● **Museum of London** - For a great walk through London history - from pre-Roman times on. Open Tuesday-Saturday 10:00-6:00, Sunday 2:00-6:00 (tube: Pimlico).

● **Victoria and Albert Museum** - surprisingly interesting collection of costumes, armour, furniture, decorative arts, and much more. Monday-Thursday and Saturday 10:00-6:00, Sunday 2:20-5:00. Closed Friday (tube: Kensington).

Entertainment and theatre

You could spend a lifetime being entertained in London. It bubbles with top-notch shows seven nights a week, reaching a boil each summer. The key to maximising your entertainment pleasure is to take advantage of 'What's On', 'City Limits', or 'Time Out' magazines, available at most newsstands. You can telephone 246-8041 for a recording of today's events. You'll choose from classical, jazz, rock and far-out music, Gilbert and Sullivan, dance, comedy, spectator sports, film and theatre.

I'd focus on the theatre. Choose from the Royal Shakespeare Company, top musicals, comedy, thrillers, sex farces, and more. Performances are nightly except Sunday, usually with one matinee a week. Matinees (listed in a box in 'What's On') are cheaper and normally not sold out.

Most theatres are in the Piccadilly-Trafalgar Square area, and are marked on tourist maps. Most theatres, box offices, hotels and tourist offices have a very handy 'Theatre Guide' brochure listing everything in town. The quickest and easiest way to get a ticket is through a ticket agency (at Victoria T.I., or scattered throughout the theatre district) but it's cheaper to go direct: call the theatre and many will hold tickets for you to be picked up an hour before the show time. If it's 'sold out' there's usually a way to get a seat. Call and ask how. If all else fails and money is no object, you can be victimised by a tout.

I usually buy the second-cheapest tickets. Most theatres are so small there's hardly a bad seat. 'Moving up' later on is less than a capital offence. The famous 'half price booth' in Leicester Square sells cheap tickets the day of the show. If you'll ever enjoy Shakespeare it'll be here by the Royal Shakespeare Company in the new Barbican Centre (tel. 628-8795).

Itinerary options - day trips from London

London is surrounded by exciting and easy day-trip destinations. Several tour companies take London-based travellers out and back every day (call Britain Shrinkers at 629-2525 or National Express at 730-0202 or Tourist Info for ideas). The British Rail system works with London as a hub and normally offers round-trip fares that cost just a little more than their already reasonable one-way fares. See British Rail's handy 'Day Trips from London' booklet.

London uses a different train station for each region. For schedule information call the appropriate station: Kings Cross — 278-2477, Liverpool Street — 283-7171, Paddington — 262-6767, all others — 928-5100.

TOUR 3
MORE OF LONDON

After finishing up any necessary business to prepare for later in the trip, we'll continue seeing the many sights of London listed in 'Tour 2'. There are many options depending on your interests. I'd do this:

Suggested Schedule

8:00 am	Breakfast, easy morning, any last tour planning or telephoning. Tube to Tottenham Court Road.
10:00 am	British Museum.
1:30 pm	Pub lunch in Fleet Street, London's frantic but dignified newspaper and print centre. Or for a light healthier meal, try 'Slender's wholefood restaurant' at 41 Cathedral Place, near St. Paul's.
2:00 pm	Walk to St. Paul's, climb to top for view. Many other Wren Churches nearby, as well as Old Bailey and the Stock Exchange.
4:00 pm	Walk to the Museum of London (open till 6:00 pm) for the best possible London history lesson.
Evening	Hopefully a performance (music or Royal Shakespeare Co.) in the new and impressive Barbican Centre a block from the London Museum. (Open until 11:00 pm daily, tel. info 638-4141 ext. 218, recorded info 628-2295).

Things to do in London

★ Reserve and pay for your hotel for your return in three weeks.
★ Reserve tickets for any special performances that are sold out now but not in three weeks (a Prom Concert in the Royal Albert Hall, tel. 589-8212, ticket to a top play like Cats, Starlight Express, Royal Shakespeare, or whatever features a big name artist).
★ Book a seat at the Stratford Theatre if the RSC is playing during your Stow-on-the-Wold stay (Tour 7).
★ Think ahead for Edinburgh Festival (August/September). Edwards & Edwards is the London ticket agency handling the festival, tel. 734-9761 (tel. 031-226-4001 in Edinburgh). If you'll hit it, reserve at least your room from London.

Specific reservations to make (especially in July and August) for this itinerary.

★ B&Bs in Bath, Stow, Iron Bridge and Ruthin. You may want to call any others deeper into the tour if you have a particular

favourite or are ready to commit yourself to a date.
★ Ruthin Medieval Banquet - book ahead.
★ Write to Tower of London (Yeoman Warden, Tower Hill, London EC3) three weeks in advance, with envelope stamped and addressed to your London hotel, requesting an invitation to the moving 'ceremony of the keys'. Say which night or nights you can come.

TOUR 4

SALISBURY, STONEHENGE, BATH

Today we pick up our car, leave the big city and tour the lively market town and cathedral of Salisbury, explore two mysterious stone circle reminders of England's ancient past - Stonehenge and Avebury - and finally get established in the price of Georgian England - Bath.

Suggested Schedule

9:00	Pick up car, drive to Salisbury
11:00	Salisbury town and cathedral. Picnic on cathedral grounds or lunch in town.
1:30	Ponder Stonehenge.
2:00	Drive to Avebury.
3:00	Don't hurry Avebury.
4:00	Lovely drive, small roads, into Bath.
5:00	Arrive, set up in Bath.

Transport

Picking up your car. London is a terrible place to drive in if you're not used to it. Survivors recommend picking up your hire car out of the city at Heathrow Airport. The tube or Airbus will take you there stresslessly, where major, eager rental agencies are lined up all trying harder. (If you decide to pick up your car in London, Kenning Car Hire (84 Holland Park Avenue, W11, tel. 727-0123) is in 'Our London Neighbourhood' next to the Holland Park tube station.)

Your hire car orientation is always rushed, but be sure to understand the basics: locate the car manual, know how to change a tyre, what kind of petrol to use, understand their breakdown policy and how to use the AA membership that comes with most car rentals. Ask the attendant for a list of drop-off offices, any map he can give you, and directions to Salisbury. Before you leave, drive around the airport car park and get to know your car for five or ten minutes. Work the keys, try everything - find problems before they find you.

★ **London - Salisbury - Stonehenge** London, like most big cities, has a ring road, the M25. Wherever you are (airport or central London) get on the M25 and follow the 'west' signs until you get to the M3. The M3 zips you toward Salisbury. After Basingstoke, take the A30 exit and you're 30 miles from Salisbury.

Market towns like Salisbury are parking nightmares. Follow signs to 'city centre' and then into a central car park.

Tour 4

From Salisbury, go to Amesbury via A345 where signs will get you to Stonehenge, 2 miles west.

Stonehenge has a free car park with public restrooms.

★ **Stonehenge - Avebury - Bath** Next, continue north from Amesbury on the A345 to the thatched village of Upavon. 'A' roads are always faster, but in this case I'd take the tiny scenic road through the villages of Hilcott, Alton Priors, and West Kennett to Avebury. You won't find a legal parking place in the village of Avebury so use the car park with the blue 'P' for tourists.

From Avebury, A4 west to Calne, A3102 south to the lovely thatched village of Sandy Lane on A342. Take the tiny lane west out of Sandy Lane to the prize-winning Tudor village of Lacock. From there, take the A4 for the most beautiful approach into Bath.

If you have a road atlas book, be sure to take advantage of its city maps. In the case of Bath, navigate by bridges and landmarks. As usual, parking in town is hopeless. Parking near your B&B shouldn't be too bad.

Sightseeing highlights

● ● **Salisbury** - Cathedral and Market - Salisbury Cathedral, marked by the tallest spire in England, is a fine reason to stop here. Admire its exterior, the cloister, the chapter with an original Magna Carta and a ring of sculptured Old Testament scenes. See how many you can identify and then ask a guard for a sheet of 'answers'.

Spend some time wandering through the old centre of town, particularly fun on market day (Saturday). We did our market chores here buying a 'brollie' (umbrella) for £2 ($3), a jumper for the nippy and wet weather, and a few cassettes for our car tape deck.

● ● **Stonehenge** - England's most famous stone circle, built 4,000 years ago in the days of Egypt's pyramids. These huge stones were brought all the way from Wales to form a remarkably accurate celestial calendar. Even today, every summer solstice (around June 21) the sun sets in just the right slot and Druids go wild. The monument is roped off so even if you pay the entry fee you're kept at a distance. While you can see it free from the road, it's worth a closer look.

● ● **Avebury** - The stone circle at Avebury is bigger, less touristy, and I think more interesting than Stonehenge. You're free to wander among 100 stones, ditches, mounds and curious patterns from the past, as well as the village of Avebury which grew up in the middle of this 1,400-foot-wide Neolithic circle. Fascinating!

TOUR 5

BATH

Bath is Europe's most underrated city. Any tour of Britain that skips Bath is sadly lacking. Two hundred years ago this city of 80,000 was the Hollywood of Britain. If ever a city enjoyed looking in the mirror — Bath's the one. It has more 'government listed' or protected historic buildings per capita than any town in England. The entire city is built of creamy warm-tone limestone called 'Bath stone'. Bath beams in its cover-girl complexion. An architectural chorus line, it's the triumph of Georgian style. Bath's narcissism is justified.

Suggested Schedule

8:15 am	Breakfast.
9:00 am	Roman baths. Double check walking tour departure time posted outside. Buy discounted combination Baths and Costume Museum ticket. Rush the museum to catch the first (and least crowded) of the guided tours which leave every 20 minutes starting at 9:20 from the actual bath (looks like a big swimming pool). You'll have 15 minutes after the tour to go back into the museum.
10:00 am	Enjoy a coffee break with the music of the Pump Room string trio in the elegant Pump Room just above the museum.
10:30 am	Take the city walking tour (depart in front of Pump Room).
12:30 pm	Your guide will probably finish at the Assembly Rooms. Drop in to find out when the Costume Museum guided tours leave and browse your way downhill into the old shopping centre to find lunch. The Royal Victoria Park nearby is ideal picnic terrain.
3:00 pm	Tour No. 1 Royal Crescent Museum.
4:00 pm	Tour the Costume Museum in the Assembly Rooms. (Adjust your afternoon schedule to make the guided tour here. The last tour is normally at 4:30.)

Sightseeing highlights

● ● ● **The Baths — Roman and Medieval** — For 2,000 years high society has enjoyed the mineral springs at Bath. Londoners travelled to 'Aquae Sulis' so often to 'take a bath' that finally the city became known as, simply, Bath. This hot water source of

Bath's greatness is a fine Roman museum with tours every 20 minutes. Only with the enthusiastic help of your guide will the complex of ancient Roman, medieval, and modern baths and buildings make sense. Buy the combined Baths and Costume Museum ticket here for a discount. Open 9:00-6:00 daily. Tours leave at 9:20, 9:40, 10:00 and so on throughout the day. In August the baths are open evenings from 8:30 to 10:30 — magical atmosphere!

● **Pump Room** — Just above the Roman baths, this elegant Georgian Hall is a visitor's best chance to be Old World elegant. Drop by for morning coffee 10:00-12:00 with a string trio, or afternoon tea 3:00-5:00 with piano entertainment. This is your opportunity to have a famous but not especially good 'Bath bun' and drink the curative water.

● ● ● **Walking tour of Bath** — These leave from the front of the Pump Room daily at 10:30 (afternoon tours as well in July and August). They are given free by local citizens who simply want to share their love of Bath with its many visitors. For a private (not free) guide call 61977, or 312901.

● ● ● **Costume Museum** in the Assembly Rooms — One of Europe's great museums displaying 300 years of fashion one frilly decade at a time. Free tours leave several times a day and the guides are great. Drop in or call to check tour times. Learn why Yankee Doodle 'stuck a feather in his cap and called it macaroni', and much more. Open 9:30-6:00, telephone (0225) 61111.

● ● **Royal Crescent** and **The Circus** — Bath is an architectural chorus line and these are the stars. These first elegant Georgian 'houses' by John Wood are well covered in the city walking tours. The corner house at No. 1 Royal Crescent, is your best look into a house from Jane Austen's day. Expensive at £2.50 ($4.50) but worthwhile to get behind all those classy exteriors. Tue-Sat 11:00-5:00, Sun 2:00-5:00, March-October only (closed Mondays).

National Centre of Photography — The only museum of its kind I've seen, exhibiting the earliest cameras and photos and their development along with temporary contemporary exhibits. 11:00-5:30 daily except Sunday off-season.

● **American Museum** — Eighteen completely furnished rooms from the 1600s to the 1800s with a guide in each room eager to fill you in on the candles, maps, bed pans, and various religious sects that make domestic American history surprisingly interesting. One room is a quilter's nirvana. Open 2:00-5:00, April to October. Closed Mondays.

The Abbey — On the main square, this is worth a look. The Abbey is 500 years old, has good fan vaulting, and is most impressive during an evensong service (schedule on the door).

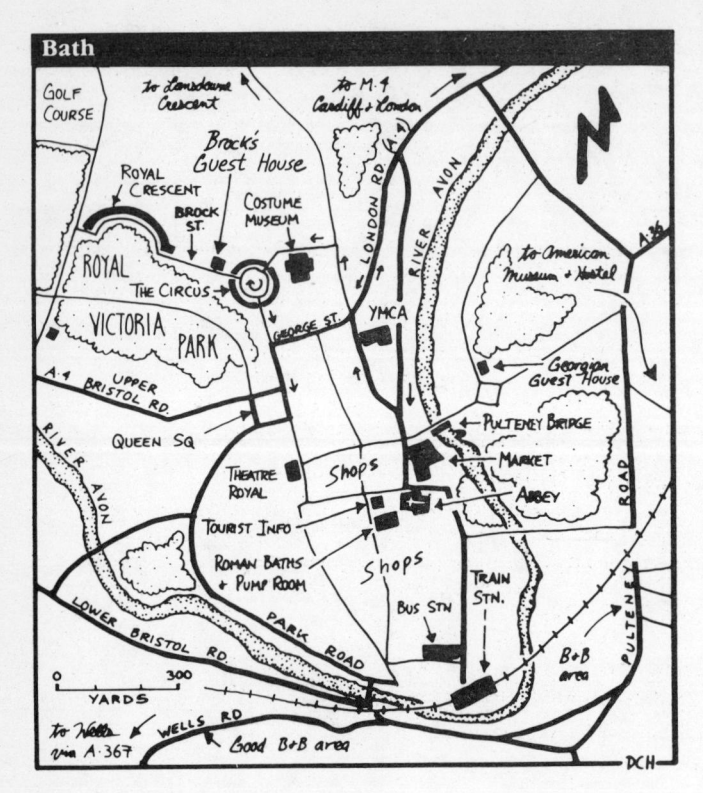

Food and accommodation

While it's one of England's most popular cities, Bath handles its crowds well. For 60p the tourist information will find you a £7 to £10 ($12-17) B&B. Midday arrivals should find a room but this is a place where I would call ahead — especially in peak season.

Brock's Guest House — If you can afford to splash out, this place is the 'cherry on the top' of your Bath visit. Marion Dodd has just restored this home built in 1765 by John Wood. It's quiet, friendly, and couldn't be better located between the Royal Crescent and the elegant Circle at 32 Brock Street. Marion charges £13 ($23) per person, with tea whenever you like, and a royal breakfast. TV in the room, launderette around the corner. Tel. (0225) 338374. Like nearly every listing in this book, she'll hold telephone reservations with no deposit until 5:00 (call if you'll be a little late). If Marion is full she can set you up in a friend's B&B nearby.

The Georgian Guest House — Run by Sybil Barry, this place is quiet, clean, very central, and — for Bath — reasonable with

B&B at £10.50 ($18) each. The rooms are nothing special and it's one of those tall skinny places — lots of stairs. Tel. 24103, 34 Henrietta Street, Bath, BA2 6LR.

For the cheapest beds, the **Youth Hostel**, tel. 65674, is very nice but not central. The **YMCA**, tel. 60471, is a bit shabby but friendly and wonderfully central on Broad Street. Doubles are £8-9 ($14-15) per person, the dormitory is cheaper at about £7 ($12).

Eating in Bath is fun. There's no shortage of places in all price ranges — just stroll around the centre of town. I've enjoyed many meals in Bath simply by strolling until I found a place that tickled that evening's fancy. For lunch, try the cafe upstairs in the **Bartlett Street Antique Centre** (downhill from the Assembly Rooms), or the **Crystal Palace Pub** with hearty meals under rustic timbers or in the sunny courtyard (just south of the Abbey. Ask around — it's a local hangout).

Helpful hints

The Pulteney Bridge and riverside parks are another pleasant aspect of Bath. Don't take the cleverly advertised but disappointing ghost walk. There's great shopping between the Abbey and the Assembly Rooms, especially the many antique shops. The 'walk and ride' tours are not as good as the free city walks. When in need, the Pump Room's toilets are always nearby and open to the discreet public. Shops close at 5:30 except on Thursdays when they stay open later.

TOUR 6
WELLS, GLASTONBURY, WOOKEY HOLE

Today, after a free morning in Bath, we swing south visiting Wells, England's smallest cathedral city; Glastonbury, steeped in legends of the Holy Grail and King Arthur; and the impressive — if a bit silly — haunted caves of Wookey Hole.

Suggested Schedule	
Morning	Free in Bath
1:00 pm	Drive to Wookey Hole.
1:30 pm	Tour Wookey Hole.
4:00 pm	Browse around Wells town and cathedral, staying for the 5:15 evensong service.
6:00 pm	Drive 5 miles to Glastonbury. Tour the Abbey, then climb the tower before sun sets. Great view and eerie feelings.
8:00 pm	Drive back to Bath, possibly stopping at a countryside pub for dinner.

Transport
This plan calls for 50 miles of driving. The roads are good, the scenery okay, but not earthshaking. I'd stick to the faster 'A' roads going as direct as possible.

In Wells, try to park on the main square next to the tourist office, post office, and just about everything else. In Glastonbury, the abbey car park is easy to find.

Sightseeing highlights
- **Wookey Hole** — This is definitely a commercial venture. It's a bit touristy but I thought worth the £3 ($6) admission for two hours of fun. Just 2 miles from Wells, Wookey Hole is a hodgepodge of entertainment starting with a wonderful guided tour of some big but mediocre caves complete with history, geology lessons and witch stories. Then you're free to wander through a traditional rag-paper-making mill with a demonstration, and into a 19th century circus room — a riot of colour, funny mirrors and a roomful of old penny arcade machines that visitors can actually play for as long as their pennies (on sale there) last. They even have old girlie shows. Finally you come to Madame Tussaud's warehouse where the now too-young face of Prince Charles and formerly-famous faces of people like Twiggy are stored waiting for I don't know what.
- ● **Wells** — This wonderfully preserved little cathedral city — England's smallest — is worth a stop. Its 13th century cathedral

complex is one of the most interesting in England. Don't miss the carving on the west front, the unique hourglass-shaped double arch, the grand chapter house, or the nearby bishop's palace. The cathedral has a good shop and a handy cafeteria. Weekdays at 5:15 the cathedral choir gives a lovely evensong service.

If you're in the mood for a picnic, drop by the aromatic Cheese Board on the market square for a great selection of tasty local cheeses. Remember, Cheddar is just down the road. I asked the lady for the most interesting mix worth a pound.

● ● **Glastonbury** — This place bubbles with legend and history. Its once grand and now ruined abbey is the supposed birthplace of Christianity in England. 500 years ago it was England's leading abbey. It's well worth a wander. The little abbey museum has an impressive reconstruction of the abbey as it was before Henry VIII got to it. The Glastonbury Tor is a conical hill, supposedly the mystical Isle of Avalon, from King Arthur's day. You can drive around the hill and park very close to its base. Walk to the summit for a marvellous view and a great 'king of the mountain' feeling. The abbey is open daily until 7:30 and the tower never closes.

Itinerary options

If you want to see the American Museum near Bath, which is only open from 2:00 to 5:00 pm, skip your free time in Bath and the evensong service in Wells, doing Glastonbury first, then Wells and Wookey Hole, arriving in Claverton outside Bath by 3:00 to see the American Museum. Or you could follow the original schedule but replace Wookey Hole with the American Museum, getting there right at 2:00.

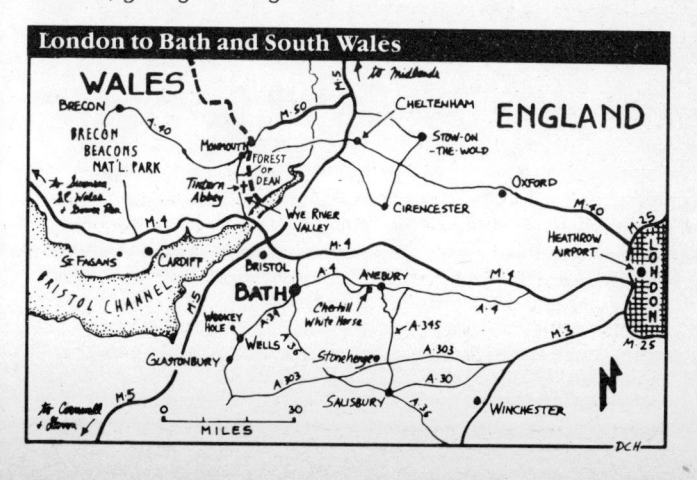

TOUR 7

SOUTH WALES, FOLK MUSEUM, WYE RIVER VALLEY

From Bath we'll dash into South Wales for a look at its capital city of Cardiff, before spending several hours exploring the past at St. Fagan's Welsh Open-Air Folk Museum. Then we'll take the scenic route past the romantic Tintern Abbey ruins, up the lush Wye River valley, through the remote Forest of Dean and into England's picturesque Cotswold Hills — establishing our headquarters in the central village of Stow-on-the-Wold.

Suggested Schedule

8:00 am	Breakfast.
8:30 am	Drive to Cardiff.
10:00 am	St. Fagan's Welsh Folk Museum. Tour grounds first, picnic, or lunch in cafeteria, then tour museum gallery.
1:00 pm	Drive to Tintern Abbey.
2:00 pm	Explore Tintern, Wye River, Forest of Dean.
5:00 pm	Drive to Stow-on-the-Wold.
6:30 pm	Set up in Stow.

Transport

Bath — Cardiff, St. Fagan's — From Bath it's 10 miles north on A46 past a little village called Philadelphia to the M4 motorway. Now only a speed reader can follow the map as you can go as fast as your car and conscience will let you. Crossing a huge suspension bridge you enter Wales. 20 miles later you're in Cardiff.

Follow the M48, then A48, then the signs right into the centre of town. You'll pass big impressive government administrative buildings and the huge old castle that dominates the heart of Wales' biggest city. After crossing the bridge, turn right on Cathedral Road (A4119) and follow the signs 4 miles further west to St. Fagan's. If you lose the trail just ask for directions.

Cardiff — Stow — From St. Fagan's get back on the M4 as soon as possible and backtrack until just before the big suspension bridge. Take the Chepstow exit and follow the signs up the A466 to Tintern Abbey and the Wye River valley. If you stop at Tintern Abbey, buy the Wye River-Cotswold Hills map. Carry on to Monmouth, and if you're running late follow the A40 and the M50 to the Tewkesbury exit where the A438 and the B4077 will zip you right in to Stow-on-the-Wold.

If you have time and energy, explore the romantic old Forest of Dean leaving the A466 for Coleford and following the green shaded 'scenic routes' through the beloved old oak forest that made Admiral Nelson's ships so strong. From Cinderford take the A48 and A40 through Cheltenham to Northleach where it's a straight ten-minute trip on the A429 to Stow.

Sightseeing highlights

Cardiff — The Welsh capital with 300,000 people and a pleasant modern centre across from the castle. The castle is worthless unless you catch one of the fun tours which leave every half hour. The interior is a Victorian fantasy.

● ● ● **St. Fagan's Welsh Folk Museum** — This is your best look at traditional Welsh folk life. Twenty old houses from all corners of this little country have been saved and reconstructed here. Each is fully furnished and in the summer comes equipped with a local expert warming herself by the toasty fire and happy to tell you anything you want to know about life in this old cottage. You'll also see traditional crafts in action and a fascinating gallery displaying crude washing machines, the earliest matches, elaborately carved 'love spoons' and even a case of memorabilia from the local man who pioneered cremation. Everything is well explained. The cafeteria is pleasant and cheap, a good lunch option. Open daily 10:00-5:00, Sundays 2:30-5:00.

● **Caerphilly Castle** — A very impressive but gutted old castle, only thirty minutes from St. Fagan's. The second largest in Europe after Windsor, it has two concentric walls and was considered to be a brilliant arrangement of defensive walls and moats. It's interesting to see how Cromwell's demolition crew tried to destroy it, creating the leaning tower of Caerphilly. Open daily 9:30-6:30. (Note: this itinerary covers other equally impressive fortresses, so you may want to skip this one to make time for the scenic drive to Stow.)

● **Tintern Abbey** — Just off the scenic A466 road in a lush natural setting, this is worth a stop. The abbey shop and local tourist information desk next door are very helpful. You can buy the Wye-Cotswolds map and 'A Tourist Guide to North Wales' here.

● **Wye River Valley** and **Forest of Dean** — Lush, mellow and historic, this region seduced me into an unexpected overnight stop. Read up on the Forest of Dean with its special dialect, strange political autonomy and its ties to Trafalgar and Admiral Nelson.

Food and accommodation — Stow-on-the-Wold

Stow-on-the-Wold is the ideal base for the Cotswolds. Whilst it has its crowds, most are day-trippers and even summer nights are peaceful. Stow has plenty of B&B options and a tourist office on the main square that can get you set up. Here are some specifics.

The Stow-Away B&B — Norman and Barbara Axon make you feel like part of the family. Only after an hour of tea and talk did I have a chance actually to bring in my bag. Opened in 1985, they are two streets off the main square (14 Park Street, Stow-on-the-Wold, Gloucestershire, tel. 31839, £8 ($14) B&B, with tea in the evening). Take the loft room if you can.

The Pound — Cosy, quaint, restored 500-year-old home of Mrs. Cartland, £10 ($17), in Sheep Street, tel. 30229.

The Malthouse — Another winner run by Brian and Cathryn Sykes along with their pottery and craft gallery, just off Sheep Street in tiny Digbeth Street, £10 ($17), tel. 31341.

The Guest House — 6 miles west of Stow in the tiny village of Guiting Power, this is your sleepy village alternative. Modern, clean, and friendly, in a 400-year-old house. £9 ($16), Post Office Lane, Guiting Power, Cheltenham, GL54 5TZ, tel. (O4515) 470, Bernie and Yvonne Sylvester.

Stow-on-the-Wold Youth Hostel — Right on the main square of Stow in an historic old building, well run, friendly atmosphere, good food served or do-it-yourself in member's kitchen, one double room for married hostellers, popular in summer. Telephone reservations (0451) 30497. £5 ($8) per night, £7 ($12) with dinner.

Other Cotswold Youth Hostels — The hostels at Cleve Hill (tel. 024267) 2065, Duntisbourne Abbots (tel. (028582) 682), and Charlbury (tel (0608) 810202) are good bases for exploring the Cotswold villages. They are special because they rent bikes for a daily charge. Call (05432) 22279 for specifics.

Pub Grub — Have dinner at the **Queen's Head** in the main square. Try their local Cotswold brew, Donnington.

Itinerary options

If you want to skip the scenic three hours of Tintern, Wye, and Dean, you could spend an hour in Cardiff and an hour at Caerphilly Castle, and take the Motorway (M4, M5) and A436 direct to Stow. Or, if you stepped up the tempo throughout, adding just a tinge of hecticity to the plan, you could sneak Caerphilly Castle into the suggested itinerary after St. Fagan's. If you need to save a day somewhere, consider skipping South Wales entirely.

For a special night check into the **St. Briavels Castle Youth Hostel** (tel. (0594) 530272. £5 ($8), you must be a Youth Hostel member). It's an 800-year-old Norman castle, used by King John in 1215, the year he signed the Magna Carta, comfortable (as castles go), friendly, and in the centre of the quiet village of St. Briavels just north of Tintern Abbey. For dinner, eat at the hostel or walk 'just down the path' to the **Crown Pub** (very friendly, with good cheap food and fine pub atmosphere).

If a restful seaside break sounds good about now, consider a side trip to Gower Peninsula (southwest of Swansea, about a ninety-minute drive from Cardiff) for a pleasant blend of farms, ancient monuments, sleepy towns, cliffs and windswept Welsh beaches. Head straight for rugged Rhossili town on the western tip of the peninsula. Among several fine walks in the area, one takes you high above the beach with great views and an opportunity to frolic with the spirit of Dylan Thomas among the lush hillsides and peaceful ponies. Rhossili has one hotel (Worms Head, tel. 390512) and several B&Bs. Try the Devon View Guest House (£8.50 ($15), tel. 390555).

TOUR 8
THE COTSWOLD VILLAGES AND BLENHEIM PALACE

Today we mix England's cosiest villages with her greatest countryside palace. The Cotswold Hills are dotted with storybook villages and the best are within easy reach of Stow-on-the-Wold. England has plenty of royal country mansions. If you had to choose just one to visit (and we do) Blenheim is it.

Suggested Schedule

8:00 am	Breakfast in Stow-on-the-Wold.
8:30 am	Drive to Chipping Campden.
9:00 am	Drive through Chipping Campden, Broadway, and Stanton, and via Cheltenham to Cirencester (park in central car park).
11:00 am	Cirencester — Corinium Museum, crafts centre, lunch in crafts centre cafeteria.
1:00 pm	Drive to Bibury via Coln St. Dennis, Coln Rogers, and Winson.
1:30 pm	Bibury — stroll the stream, cottages, church.
2:30 pm	Drive to Blenheim via Burford, Witney, and Woodstock (A4095).
3:15 pm	Park at palace and line up for the hour tour of Blenheim Palace.
5:15 pm	Drive to Stow-on-the-Wold via Chipping Norton.
6:00 pm	Evening stroll around Stow centre, find a good pub for dinner.

The Cotswolds
Like many fairytale regions of Europe, the present day beauty of the Cotswolds is explained by economic ups and downs. The area grew rich on the wool trade and built lovely towns and houses. Then foreign markets stole their trade and they slumped — too poor even to be knocked down. The forgotten time-passed villages have now been discovered by us 20th-century romantics, and the Cotswold villages are enjoying a new prosperity.

Transport
While distances are very small in the Cotswolds, so are the roads. Including the 20-mile drive to Blenheim, we'll probably put in 100 miles today — most of it as joyful as touring can be. Don't bumble around without a good map — any shop can sell you a fine tourist-orientated map of the region. No Cotswold town is

Tour 8

big enough to cause any problems except for peak season parking in Broadway and Bourton. Blenheim Palace is in the town of Woodstock on the A34, 7 miles northwest of Oxford. The palace turnoff is right in the town, not well signposted. By the way, a 'quick swing into Oxford' won't work — it has the worst traffic and parking problems in England. Today's theme is to take the tiny roads.

Sightseeing highlights

- **Stow-on-the-Wold** — Eight roads converge on Stow but none interrupt the peacefulness of its main square. The town has no real sights other than itself. There are several good pubs, some pleasant shops and a handy little walking tour brochure called 'Town Trail' (15p, sold at Youth Hostel counter). Put yourself in the stocks on the green and ponder our saying 'he was the laughing stock of the town'.
- **Cirencester** — 1,800 years ago this was the ancient Roman city, Corinium. It's found 20 miles from Stow down the A429 or, in Roman times, down Fosse Way. In Cirencester don't miss the Corinium Museum (open 10:00-6:00, Sundays 2:00-6:00) to find out why they say 'if you scratch Gloucestershire you'll find Rome'. The craft centre and workshops entertain visitors with traditional weaving, baking, potting, etc in action. There's also an interesting gallery and a great cafeteria. Friday is market day in Cirencester.

Cotswold Farming and Prison Museum — 9 miles south of Stow, just off the Fosse Way (A429) at Northleach. Worthwhile if you're interested in old farming machines (no crowd problems...ever).

Bourton-on-the-Water — 4 miles south of Stow. I can't figure out if they call this the 'Venice of the Cotswolds' because of its quaint canals, its miserable crowds, or just to make more money. It's too cute, worth a drive through but no more.

Broadway — 9 miles northwest of Stow. Another very crowded town, worth a drive-through but not a stop...there won't be a parking place anyway.

- **Chipping Campden** — 9 miles north of Stow. This is a close second to Stow for the best base. A real working market town, home of some incredibly beautiful thatched roofs and the richest Cotswold wool merchants ('Cotswold' comes from the Saxon phrase 'hills of sheeps coats'). Pleasant for a walk.
- ● **Snowhill** and **Stanton** — Both 2 miles south of Broadway. These two towns, along with Upper and Lower Slaughter (3 miles south of Stow) are my nominations for the most lovely Cotswold villages. All are nestled in equally beautiful countryside.
- **Bibury** — 6 miles northeast of Cirencester. This is an entertaining town with a trout farm, Cotswolds museum, stream thriving with huge trout and proud ducks, a row of very old

Cotswold Villages

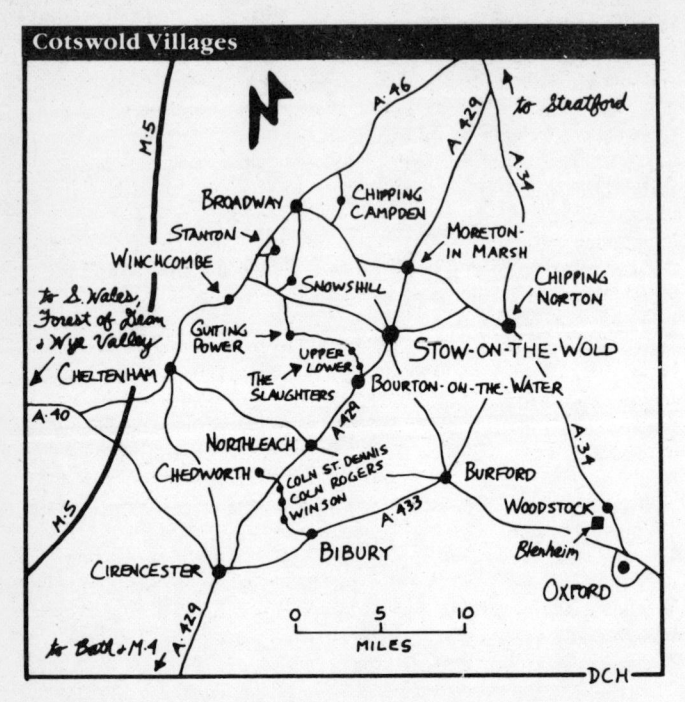

weavers' cottages, and a church surrounded by rose trees — each tended by a volunteer of the parish. Don't miss the scenic drive from Bibury to the A429 through the villages of Winson, Coln St. Dennis and Coln Rogers.

● ● ● **Blenheim Palace** — It's easy to overdo English palaces, so this tour chooses just the best. The Duke of Marlborough's home is still lived in, which is wonderfully obvious as you tour it. Churchill was born prematurely while his mother was at a Blenheim Palace party (truly a man before his time). The palace is well organised; only guided tours are allowed. They take place every ten minutes, last an hour, cost around £3 ($5). There's an excellent new Churchill exhibition which is worth lingering over, so skip to the next tour group if you need more time here. The palace is open from March through to October, 11:00-6:00, last tour leaves at 5:00.

Tour 8

Itinerary options

For a more leisurely day, skip Chipping Campden and Broadway and call at Upper and Lower Slaughter and Bourton-on-the-Water as you drive down to Cirencester. You could drive through Chipping Campden and Broadway on your way to Stratford tomorrow morning.

Remember, you're just 30 miles from Stratford, Shakespeare's birthplace. The world's best Shakespeare is performed by the Royal Shakespeare Company there and in London. You'll probably need to get your tickets in advance (in London on the first day of your trip), but if you're a Shakespeare fan, it's well worth the trouble.

If you prefer Oxford to Cambridge (which is reasonable even if I don't), you can do it as a side trip from London or from Stow-on-the-Wold. Consider an extra day in the itinerary here which would give you a whole day in the Cotswolds and a day split between Blenheim and Oxford (11:00 Blenheim tour, in Oxford by 1:00, get straight to the tourist office to reserve a spot on an afternoon city walking tour).

Consider renting a bike for a more intimate look at the Cotswolds where, according to some, two hours on two wheels is worth two days on four. There's no bike rental in Stow, but Teagues in Bourton-on-the-Water (High Street, tel. 20248) rents bikes for 75p per hour. The Slaughters are a fun bike ride away. Plan a picnic.

TOUR 9

STRATFORD UPON AVON, WARWICK CASTLE, AND COVENTRY CATHEDRAL TO IRONBRIDGE GORGE

Today we travel north into the cradle of the Industrial Revolution stopping en route at Shakespeare's birthplace in Stratford. We'll also tour England's greatest medieval castle in Warwick and visit Coventry and its cathedral, the symbol of the destruction of World War II, the determination to rebuild and the hope for peace and reconciliation. Then we zoom (hopefully) through England's second largest city, Birmingham, and into the valley of the Severn River, once churning with industry and now a land of sleepy smokestacks, soothing natural beauty and a distinct Shropshire brand of hospitality.

Suggested Schedule

8:30 am	Leave Stow-on-the-Wold.
9:15 am	Park in Stratford.
9:30 am	See the 'World of Shakespeare' show.
10:00 am	Walk around town, visit Shakespeare house.
12:00	Drive to Warwick (picnic in car or leave Stratford early and lunch at the castle).
12:30 pm	Tour castle.
2:30 pm	Drive to Coventry.
2:45 pm	Tour new and old Cathedral, visitor's centre and wander around Coventry.
5:00 pm	Drive to Ironbridge Gorge.
6:30 pm	Arrive in Ironbridge Gorge.

Transport

Today's sights are close together and served by fine roads. There's no joyriding in this plan, as we'll drive directly from each stop to the next. From Stow, drive 20 miles north on the A429 and A34 to Stratford. In Stratford cross the bridge and you're in the centre. Take the immediate left and park as close to the big modern theatre as you can.

It's only 8 miles to Warwick along the A46. The castle is well sign-posted, just south of town to the right of the main road.

Tour 9

After Warwick, follow the signs to Coventry (still on A46), and in Coventry follow signs to 'city centre' and then to 'cathedral'. The cathedral is hard to see so just look for signs. When you get to what looks like a large bus station, park in the multi-storey 'cathedral car park'.

From the cathedral follow signs through lots of sprawl to the M6 and you're on your way. The M6 will take you right through giant Birmingham. Our plan takes you through during rush hour but it doesn't seem to be a problem. From the M6 take the new M54 to the Telford/Iron Bridge exit. Iron Bridge signs will take you through a long series of roundabouts until you're there.

Sightseeing highlights

Stratford upon Avon — This is the most overrated tourist magnet in England, but we're passing through, and nobody at home would understand if we skipped Shakespeare's house.

Shakespeare's home town is blanketed with opportunities for 'bardolotry'. Only his birthplace in Henley Street is worth a visit on our itinerary. You'll enter through a modern 'Shakespeare Centre' which has little to offer besides some fine BBC theatre costumes, clean toilets and a high-tech cash register which from 9:00-6:00 daily will relieve you of around £2 ($3).

'The World of Shakespeare' shows (25 minutes) go on the half-hour, located between the big Theatre and the bridge.

If you need a room in Stratford, try the Carlton Guest House, 22 Evesham Place. Pam and David Newberry charge £11 ($20) in this clean and friendly B&B.

● ● **Royal Shakespeare Company** — The RSC is undoubtedly the best Shakespeare Company on earth. They split their season between London and Stratford. If you're a Shakespeare fan, see if the RSC schedule works into your itinerary while you're in London at the start of your trip. It's easy to make a Stratford show from Stow-on-the-Wold, or in London before you finally return home. You'll probably need to buy your tickets in advance. Box office tel. 292271, Info tel. 69191.

● ● ● **Warwick Castle** — England's finest medieval castle is well organised to give its hordes of visitors a good value for the steep entry fee (around £3.50 ($6)). Situated above the Avon River with a lush grassy moat and fairytale fortification, Warwick will entertain you from dungeon to lookout. There's something for every taste — a fine and educational armoury, a terrible torture chamber, a knight in shining armour posing on a horse, an 1898 game of statue-maker — and a grand garden and park patrolled by peacocks that's ideal for a picnic.

Cotswolds to Iron Bridge

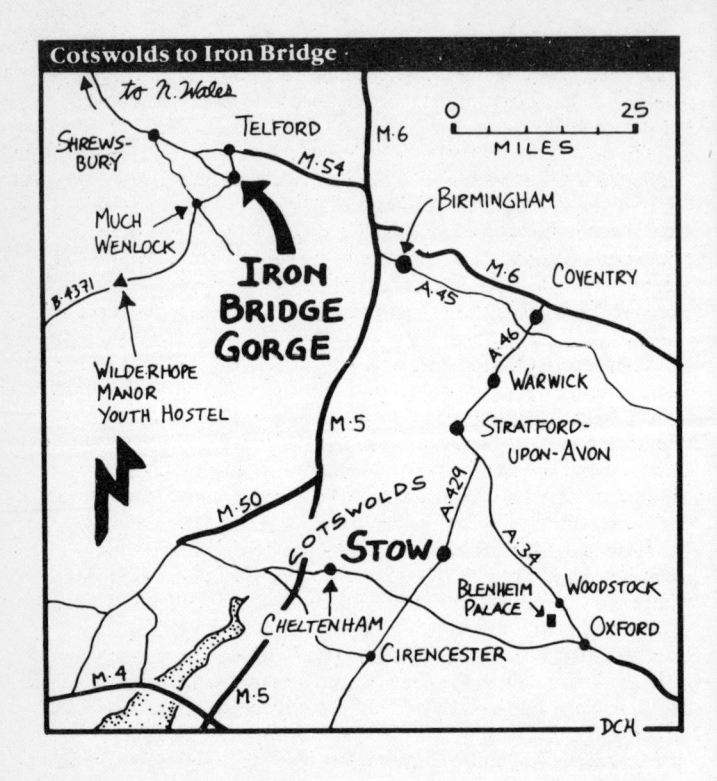

[Map showing route from Cotswolds to Iron Bridge Gorge, with locations including Shrewsbury, Telford, Much Wenlock, Wilderhope Manor Youth Hostel, Birmingham, Coventry, Warwick, Stratford-upon-Avon, Stow, Cheltenham, Cirencester, Blenheim Palace, Woodstock, and Oxford. Scale: 0-25 miles. Signed DCH.]

●● **Coventry's Cathedral** — The Germans bombed Coventry to smithereens in 1940. From that point on the word for 'to smash a place to pieces' was to 'coventrate'. But Coventry rose from the ashes, and its message to our world is one of forgiveness and reconciliation. The symbol of Coventry is the bombed out hulk of its old cathedral with the brilliant new one adjoining it. The complex is designed for visitors. Climb the tower, pick up a guided walk brochure, savour the powerful modern art, search for the symbolism, ask a hostess about the 'Community of the Cross of Nails', see the Visitors Centre (£1.50 ($2.50) donation to the church, daily 9:30-6:00, Sunday 12:00-6:00) with its award-winning 18 minute film 'The Spirit of Coventry'. Have tea and scones in the cafeteria.

Accommodation

The Ironbridge Gorge is a young attraction and doesn't have a lot of accommodation, but these are good:

The Tontine Hotel — Centrally located, exactly across from the Iron Bridge itself. It's old (1784), brick, historic, and a bit musty — in keeping with the style of the valley. For £14 ($25) each you'll get a very nice room, traditional breakfast, hotel-type service, and a helpful management happy to give sightseeing advice (tel. 2127).

The Hill View Farm — Mrs. Hawkins runs a peaceful, clean, and friendly farmhouse B&B in a great rural setting overlooking the ruins of an old abbey. Real value for £8 ($14). Address: Buildwas, Ironbridge, Shropshire; tel. 2228. Located halfway between Ironbridge and Much Wenlock — leave Ironbridge past the huge modern power plants (coal, not nuclear, but ominous nonetheless), cross the bridge and go about a mile. You'll see the sign.

Wilderhope Manor Youth Hostel — The beautifully remote and haunted 500-year-old manor house is one of my favourite youth hostels anywhere in Europe. One day a week tourists actually pay to see what we youth hostellers sleep in for £4 ($7). Six and a half miles from Much Wenlock down the B4371 towards Church Stretton. Tel. (06943) 363. Evening meal served at 7:00 pm.

Ironbridge Gorge Youth Hostel — Built in 1859 as the Coalbrookdale Institute, this grand hostel is a 20-minute walk from the Iron Bridge, down the A4169 towards Wellington. Tel. (095245) 3281.

Other B&Bs in Ironbridge Gorge: Mrs. Reed's Severn Lodge (New Road, Ironbridge, Shropshire, TF8 7AX, tel. 2148, £10 ($17)), Mrs. Roberts (Woodland Grange, 48 Lincoln Hill, tel. 2309), Mrs. Bowdler (Vine Cottage, 45 Lincoln Hill, tel. 3767), Mrs. Pearce (The Grove, New Road, tel. 3218), Mrs. Gilbride (Paradise House, Coalbrookdale, tel. 3379), Mrs. Tyley (Wren's Nest Cottage, 45 Newbridge Road, tel. 3061), Mrs Heath (Coalbrookdale Villa, Paradise, Coalbrookdale, tel. 3450).

TOUR 10
IRONBRIDGE GORGE MUSEUMS – NORTH WALES

Today we'll go from the gritty pits of England's industrial infancy to the poetic hills of remote northern Wales. The Industrial Revolution started in England's Severn River valley. Today this area is preserved as a showcase of the days that boosted England into world leadership.

Suggested Schedule

8:30 am	Breakfast.
9:30 am	Iron Bridge, town, shops.
10:00 am	Severn Warehouse, intro video, exhibition.
11:00 am	Museum of Iron, Darby's furnace, 'Rosehill', Darby's House.
12:00	Blist's Hill Museum, picnic, cafeteria or pub lunch.
3:30 pm	Drive to Wales.
4:30 pm	Llangollen, 30-minute stop in town or at abbey.
5:00 pm	Horseshoe Pass Road to Ruthin.
6:00 pm	Check in the Ruthin B&B.
7:30 pm	Medieval Banquet at Ruthin Castle.
11:00 pm	Find your way home.
Midnight	Still not home? More mead!

Ironbridge Gorge
In its glory days this now-sleepy village gave the world the first iron wheels, trains, cast iron bridge and steam locomotives and powered Britain to the pinnacle of the industrial world.

Sightseeing highlights
● ● ● **Ironbridge Gorge Industrial Revolution Museums**—Start with *the* Iron Bridge. The first ever (1779), this is the area's centrepiece, open all the time and free.

The Severn Warehouse 200 yards up stream is the orientation centre. Be here at 10:00 when it opens to see the intro film, see its exhibition, buy your guidebook and tickets (£3.95 ($7) for the whole area).

Just up the road in Coalbrookdale is the Museum of Iron (worth a quick look), Darby's first blast furnace and his house, 'Rosehill'. It was here, in 1709, that Abraham Darby first smelted iron using coke as fuel. If you're like me, 'coke' is a drink and 'smelt' is the past tense of smell, but this event kicked off the modern industrial age.

Tour 10

Iron Bridge Gorge

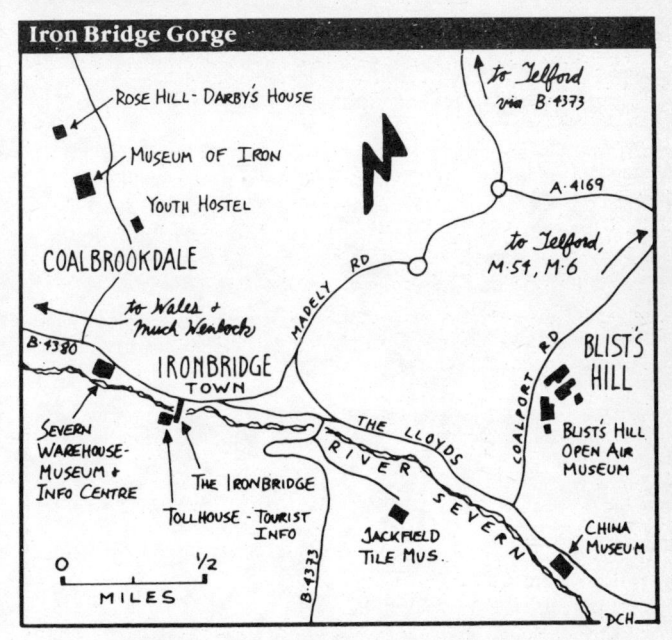

[Map showing Iron Bridge Gorge area with labels: Rose Hill - Darby's House, Museum of Iron, Youth Hostel, Coalbrookdale, to Telford via B-4373, A-4169, to Telford M·54, M·6, to Wales & much Wenlock, B-4380, Ironbridge Town, Madely Rd, Blist's Hill, Blist's Hill Open Air Museum, Severn Warehouse-Museum & Info Centre, The Ironbridge, Tollhouse - Tourist Info, The Lloyds, River Severn, Coalport Rd, Jackfield Tile Mus., China Museum, B-4373, Miles scale 0 - ½]

Save most of your time and energy for the great Blist's Hill Open Air Museum — 50 acres of Victorian industry, factories, and a recreated community from the 1890s complete with shoe makers, ancient dentist's chair, candle makers, a working pub, a fascinating squatter's cottage and a noisy slip-slidey pigsty. Take the lovely walk along the canal to the inclined plane, have a picnic or visit the cafeteria near the squatter's cottage. Buy the guidebook for a good step-by-step rundown. Open 10:00-6:00 daily. Info tel. (095245) 3522, or 3418 on weekends.

Transport — Ironbridge to Wales

Most of the day is spent at easy-to-find museums within a few miles of the Ironbridge. In mid-afternoon we'll drive for an hour to Wales via A548 through Shrewsbury, crossing the border at the cute castle town of Chirk. There take the A5 to Llangollen. Cross the bridge in Llangollen, turn left and follow the A542 and A525 past the romantic Valle Crucis Abbey, over the scenic Horseshoe Pass, and into Ruthin.

Sightseeing highlights — North Wales

Llangollen — Well worth a stop, Llangollen is famous for its International Eisteddfod (July 1-10), a festival of folk songs and dance, very popular — and crowded. You can walk or take a horse-drawn boat down its old canal towards the lovely 13th-century Cistercian Abbey near the even older and more thought-provoking old cross called Eliseg's Pillar. You'll at least glimpse all these things from the A542 on your way up the exciting Horseshoe Pass.

Ruthin — The ideal base for your exploration of North Wales. Ruthin (pron: Rithin) is a market town serving the scenic Vale of Clwyd (pron: Kluid). Each Wednesday is Medieval Day as the square dresses up and everything goes traditional (10:00-5:00 in summer). The Tourist Info Office (10:00-5:00 daily, tel. (08242) 3992) can give you plenty of info and book reservations for rooms and the medieval banquet. Located in a busy crafts centre with 14 working shops, a gallery and a fine cafeteria, the place bubbles with small town community spirit.

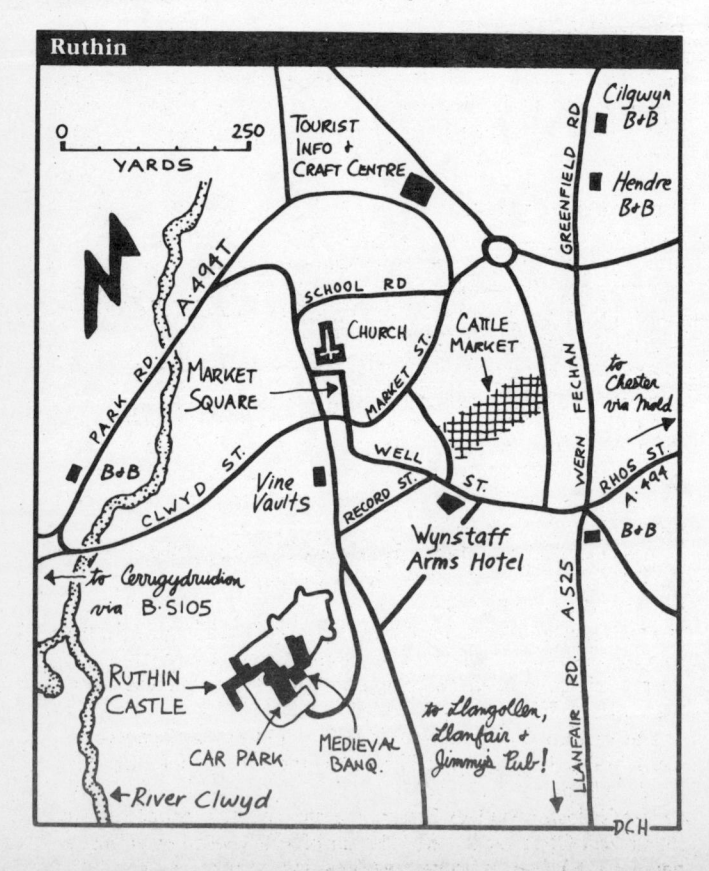

● ● **The Ruthin Castle Medieval Banquet** — By most
accounts, this is Britain's best 'medieval banquet'. Of course, it's a
touristy gimmick — but what a *fun* one. For one crazy evening I
chose to accept this romanticised trip into the bawdy Welsh past.
English, Scottish, Irish and Welsh medieval banquets are all
variations on the same theme. This one is more tasteful and less
expensive than most — and it plays right into our itinerary.

You'll start off with a chunk of bread dipped in salt which the
maiden mentions will 'guarantee your safety'. Your medieval
master of ceremonies then seats you and the evening of food,
drink, and music rolls gaily on. Harp music, angelic singing,
mead, spiced wine, four hearty traditional courses eaten with
your fingers and a dagger, bibs, candle light, pewter goblets and
lots of entertainment including insults slung at the Irish, Scots,
English and brash colonials.

These banquets cost around £15 ($25), start at 7:30 nearly
every evening and usually sell out (well in advance on Friday and
Saturday evenings). Telephone your reservation at (08242) 3435.
The castle is just down Castle Street from the town square, easy
parking at the doorstep.

Accommodation

Cilgwyn is a elegant old house run by busy Mrs. Hunter (who
also has a big shop on the main square). The place has a view, a
comfy lounge, fine breakfasts and a classy but make-yourself-at-
home atmosphere. On Greenfield Road, the first left in the
direction of 'Mold' past the Tourist Information and craft
centre — just a 5-minute walk from T.I. and 10 minutes from the
town square and castle. Tel. 4486. £9 ($15).

Hendre is just before you get to Cilgwyn, also on Greenfield
Road. Mr. & Mrs. King run this place in a way that makes you
part of the family immediately. Mr. King is happy to help with
sightseeing ideas. The house is small, modern, clean. TV in each
room. £9 ($15). Tel. 4078.

Mrs. Beryl Jones' Farm House B&B, at Bryn Awel,
Bontuchel, tel. (08242) 2481, small, friendly, lovely setting just
outside of town, £8 ($14).

The Wine Vaults is an old inn right on Ruthin's main square.
Run by Mrs. Taylor, pub downstairs, most central location, great
guests' lounge, modern plumbing. A little musty and less cosy
than a B&B. Tel. 2067, £10 ($17).

The Ruthin Castle is the ultimate in old world elegance for
North Wales. It's worth the £25 ($40) they charge for B&B Tel.
(08242) 2664.

Hiker's Hostel **Nant-yr-Hafod** is a simple stone cottage just off
the ancient Offa's Dyke Path. Not an official youth hostel, just a
handy £3 ($5) bed for budget travellers. Two dormitories and a

double, ½ mile off A525, 6 miles before Ruthin, turn at Plough Inn. Address: Hafod Bilston, Llandegla Wrexham, Clwyd, tel. (097888) 693.

Food
Pub Grub: The **White Horse Inn** in the village of Llanfair, 2 miles south of Ruthin on the A525 has great food and a friendly atmosphere, well-stocked with Welsh friends, fun pool-and-darts room. Jimmy runs the place, spending more time mingling than behind the bar.

Itinerary options
If you're not into heavy metal, leave the Ironbridge museums early after lunch (skip the Museum of Iron, doing just the Blist's Hill Museum) and take a scenic detour from Iron Bridge south along Wenlock Edge (B4368) for the best Shropshire scenery. Use the 95p Shropshire guide available at any local tourist office. Drive from Clun, wind up to Welshpool and from there to Llangollen for a longer stop.

Also, if you can't do the medieval banquet tonight, try to book it for tomorrow. If you didn't buy the North Wales guide in South Wales, get it in Llangollen.

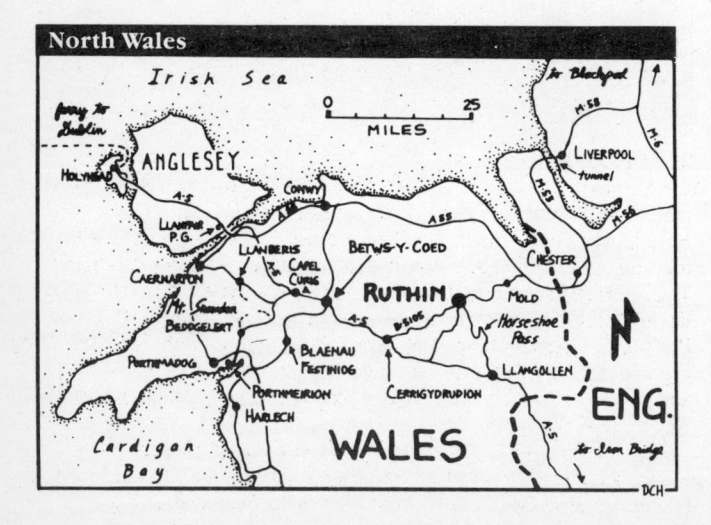

TOUR 11
EXPLORING NORTH WALES

Variety is the spice of travel and our day includes: a tour of Caernarfon, North Wales' mightiest castle; one of the world's largest slate mines at Blaenau Ffestiniog; and some of Britain's most beautiful scenery in the Snowdonia National Park, driving around the towering Snowdon through lush forests and desolate moor country.

Suggested Schedule

8:30 am	Breakfast (earlier if possible).
9:00 am	Drive to Caernarfon with short stops in Penmachno Mill, Betws-y-Coed (info centre, shops or waterfalls), and over Llanberis Mountain Pass.
11:30 am	Arrive at Caernarfon, picnic on waterfront.
12:00	Caernarfon Castle. Catch 12:00 tour, 1:00 film in Eagle Tower, 1:30 climb to top for view.
2:00 pm	Walk through town, shop, see Regimental Museum or Prince of Wales Exhibition in castle.
2:30 pm	Drive scenic road to Blaenau Ffestiniog.
3:30 pm	Tour Llechwedd Slate Mines.
5:30 pm	Drive home via Denbigh.
7:00 pm	Arrive in Ruthin. Dinner (with Jimmy) in White Horse Inn in Llanfair.

Transport

Every road in North Wales has its charm, but this day includes the best — lots of scenic touring on small roads. Take the little B5105 road out of Ruthin to Cerrigydrudion (down the steepest road off the main square and follow the signs to Cerrigydrudion). Then follow the A5 into Betws-y-Coed with a possible quick detour to the Penmachno Woollen Mill (one mile south on B4406, well signposted). At Chapel Curig take A4086 over the rugged Pass of Llanberis, just under the summit of Snowdon, and on to Caernarfon. Park under the castle (very central) in the harbourside car park.

The A4085 from Caernarfon southeast through Beddgelert to Penrhyndendraeth is lovely. Make things even more beautiful by taking the little B4410 road from Garreg to Maentwrog. Go through the depressing and dark mining town of Blaenau Ffestiniog on A470 until you wind up into the hills of slate and turn right into the Llechwedd Slate Mine.

After the mine, the A470 continues north into the most scenic stretch of all (several remote and intriguing B&Bs if you decide to spend the night) through Dolwyddelan and back to the A5 which you'll take for 6 miles east before following the winding, windy A543 road over the stark moors to Denbigh (drive up to the castle for a fine view). From Denbigh you're a 15-minute journey to Ruthin.

Sightseeing highlights

Betws-y-Coed — This is the resort centre of the Snowdonia National Park, with more than its share of tour buses and souvenir shops. It has a good National Park and Tourist Information office. The main street is worth a walk. Two miles south of town is the Penmachno Woollen Mill — just 1 mile off the A5, free, and surprisingly interesting. On the other side of town (you'll see the car park a mile down the A5) are Swallow Falls. Depending on where you come from, these are also worth a linger. (5 minute walk from road.)

● ● **Caernarfon Castle** — Edward I built this impressive castle 700 years ago to establish English rule over North Wales. It's a great castle, all ready to entertain. See the film (on the half hour in the Eagle Tower), climb the Eagle Tower for a great view, take the guided tour (50 minutes, included in admission price, on the hour from centre of courtyard in front of the entrance) and see the special exhibition on the investiture of Prince Charles and earlier Princes of Wales.

● **Llechwedd Slate Mine Tour** — Slate mining played a huge role in the Welsh heritage and this mine on the north of the bleak mining town of Blaenau Ffestiniog does its best to explain the mining culture of Wales. This is basically a romanticised view of the depressing existence of the Welsh miners of the Victorian age who put the slate roofs on most of Europe. Wales has a poor economy, so tourist-ising slate mines is understandable. Open 10:00-6:00 daily, tours £2.15/£3.25 ($4/$5.50), tel. (0766) 830306. Take the 'deep mine' tour, dress warmly, don't miss the slate-splitting demonstration.

Helpful hints

The Welsh language is alive and well. In a pub, impress your friends (or make some) by toasting the guy who may have just bought your drink. Say 'Yuchk-eh dah' (meaning 'good health to you') and 'Dee och' ('thank you') or 'Dee och on vowr' ('thanks very much').

TOUR 12
BLACKPOOL, ENGLAND'S PLAYGROUND

Today we go from God's glorious garden to Man's tacky glittering city of fun, from pristine North Wales to the bells and lights of Blackpool. Blackpool, a middle-sized city with a six-mile beach promenade, is ignored by guidebooks (*Let's Go: Britain* in 500 pages of small print never even mentions Blackpool), and even the most thorough bus tour will show you castles till your ears crenellate but never take a visitor to Blackpool.

This is Britain's fun puddle where every Englishman goes — but none will admit it. It's England's most visited attraction, the private domain of its working class. It's the place local widows and workers go year after year to escape. Tacky and lowbrow, perhaps — but it's still part of English national life and that's why we're going.

Our plan is to enjoy a slow morning in Ruthin, drive two hours, find somewhere to stay and spend the rest of the day just 'muckin' about'. If you're bored in Blackpool, you're tired of life.

Suggested Schedule	
9:00 am	Breakfast, slow morning.
10:00 am	Ruthin, free time, craft centre, shopping.
11:00 am	Drive to Blackpool, picnic en route.
1:00 pm	Blackpool. Visit tourist office (follow signs) and find a B&B, buy show ticket, catch a tram to the South Pier.
2:00 pm	Pleasure Beach.
4:30 pm	The Blackpool Tower.
7:30 pm	Old Time Music Hall Show.
10:00 pm	Prowl through the night lights, people, one armed bandits, pubs and clubs.

Transport

You'll be amazed how fast the motorway will get you to Blackpool. From Ruthin take the A494 through the town of Mold and follow the blue signs to the motorway. The M56 will zip you to the M6 where you'll turn north towards Preston and Lancaster. After Preston take the M55 right into Blackpool and drive as close as you can to the stubby Eiffel-type tower in their town centre. From here you're a short walk to the tourist office and to the B&B district around Albert Road. Park carefully; petty vandals abound.

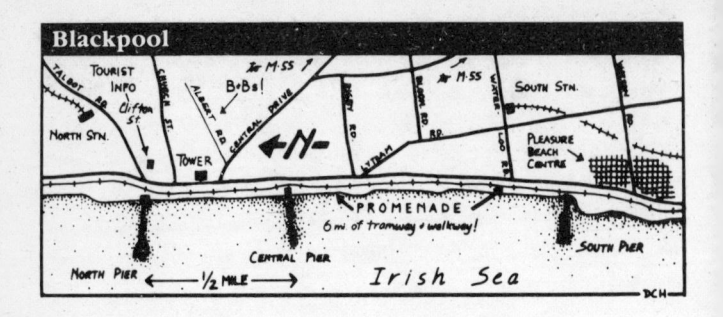

Sightseeing highlights

Tourist Info Office — First of all, go to the helpful T.I. Get the city map (20p), pick up brochures about all the amusement centres, and go over your plans. Ask about special shows and evening events and for advice on rooms.

Remember, Blackpool is second only to London as a centre for live theatre.

● **Blackpool Tower** — Much more than just a tower, this is a giant fun centre. You pay £2.50 ($4.50) to get in, and after that the fun is free. Working your way up from the bottom, visit the fascinating aquarium, the bad house of silly horrors, the very elegant ballroom with live music and dancing all day, the dance of discovery (funny mirrors and lots of hands-on curiosities — don't miss the 'Meet Your Friends' chamber and the robot that will actually verbalise whatever you type). The finale is the tower. This symbol of Blackpool is a stubby version of its more famous Parissian cousin. Still, the view from the top is smashing, especially at sunset. Consider a coffee break before leaving to watch the golden oldies dance to the grand pipe organ in the ballroom.

Tram cars — Survey Blackpool's 6-mile beach promenade from a vintage tram car. They go up and down the waterfront constantly and make much more sense than driving.

The Gypsie Rosalee type spiritualists — a fixture at Blackpool. I was told I 'mustn't leave without having my fortune told' but, at £2.50 per palm, I'll read them myself.

● ● **Old Time Music Hall Show** — There are many shows at Blackpool but its speciality is the old-fashioned variety that went out with vaudeville. These are a great hit with 'Twirlies' (senior citizens, infamous for using their bus passes 'too-early' before rush hour fades). It's definitely a corny show — neither hip nor polished — but it's fascinating to be surrounded by hundreds of partying British seniors, swooning again, waving their hankies to the predictable beat, and giggling at jokes I'd never tell my grandma. Bus loads of happy widows come from all corners of England to enjoy an 'Old Time Music Hall Show'. Buy your ticket in the afternoon, about £3.50 ($6), ask a local for the best show, probably on a pier. Try for Mike Donohoe's 'Great Days of Music Hall' show.

'The Illuminations' — Every September and October Blackpool stretches its season by 'illuminating' its 6-mile seafront with countless lights all blinking and twinkling to the delight of those who visit this electronic festival. Part of me kept saying 'I've seen bigger and I've seen better' but I shut up and just had some simple fun like everyone on my specially decorated tram.

● **Pleasure Beach** — These 42 acres of rides (over 80, including 'the best selection of big thrill rides in Europe'), ice skating shows, cabarets, and amusements attract six million people a year, making it England's most popular attraction.

● ● **People watching** — Blackpool's top sight is its people. You'll see England here like nowhere else. Grab someone's hand, a big stick of 'candy floss' and stroll.

Accommodation

Blackpool is in the business of accommodating people who can't afford to go to Spain. Simple B&Bs and hotels abound. The classy expensive hotels are, predictably, along the seafront. Countless lacklustre budget alternatives cluster, very handy and central, around Albert Road, near the Central Pier and the tower. These B&Bs almost all have the same design — minimal character, maximum number of beds. Double rooms (in the six or seven places I visited) are all the same small size with a small double bed, your basic English breakfast and a decent shower down the hall. Prices range from £8 ($14) (dingy) to £10 ($17) (cheery) per person.

Arriving at midday, you should have no trouble finding a place. Mid-July to mid-August and summer weekends are most crowded. I stayed at the Pickwick Hotel, 93, Albert Road, Blackpool FY1 4PW, tel. (0253) 24229, £9 ($16)/person. It was clean, friendly and cheery enough but nothing special.

Itinerary options

I skip Chester on this itinerary — it's a second rate York. But, many people love old Chester, and we drive right by it today. If you leave Ruthin at 9:00 you could have a good two-hour look at Chester. If you'd like an especially big dose of tack you could go right to Blackpool and dive in.

Liverpool, a gritty but surprisingly enjoyable city, is a fascinating stop en route to Blackpool if you're a Beatles fan or would like to look urban England straight in its problem-plagued, not-a-fairy-tale-in-sight eyes.

From Ruthin get to the M53 which tunnels under the Mersey River. Once in town follow the signs to Pier Head and park just past the huge and curiously named Royal Liver Building in the Maritime Museum car park (£1.50 all day, safe, includes £1 admission to museum).

The interesting Maritime Museum, cornerstone of a huge urban renewal project, tells the Liverpool story — ships, immigrations, hard times and good times. Nearby are plenty of lively shops and restaurants.

Beatle fans will want to explore Mathew Street a few blocks away (including the famous but boarded-up Cavern Club and the Beatles Shop at No. 31). 'Beatle City' in nearby Seal Street is a new museum telling the exciting story of John, Paul, George and Ringo.

Another Liverpool attraction is its people. Be sure to break the conversational ice and get to know a Liverpudlian before you drive north along the waterfront following signs to the M58, then M6 and finally M55 into the day's second pool — Blackpool.

TOUR 13
THE LAKE DISTRICT

Blackpool to the Cumbrian Lake District is another great contrast. After a short two-hour drive we'll be in the heart of Wordsworth Country. If you never were a poet, here's your chance in a land where nature rules and man keeps a wide-eyed but low profile. Today we'll get orientated in the Lake District, enjoying a boat ride and the best six-mile walk it has to offer, before getting set up in the most remote and scenic accommodation of the trip.

Suggested Schedule

9:00 am	Breakfast (earlier if possible — unlikely in Blackpool).
9:30 am	Drive north.
11:00 am	Brockhole National Park Visitors Centre. Orientation film, then get map and guide, talk to info man, browse through exhibits, picnic in grounds or lunch in cafeteria.
1:00 pm	Drive to Ullswater, park at Glenridding.
1:45 pm	Buy boat ticket.
2:00 pm	Catch boat.
2:35 pm	Hike from Howtown to Glenridding.
5:30 pm	Drive to B&B.

Transport

Follow the M55 and M6 Motorways north from Blackpool past Lancaster, exiting on the A591 through Kendal and the town of Windermere to the Brockhole National Park Centre, half-way between Windermere and Ambleside on the A591. From Brockhole take the tiny road northeast directly to Troutbeck, and then follow the A592 to the town of Glenridding and lovely Ullswater. Just before Glenridding, turn right to the car park and boat dock (40p self-service parking stickers). We'll catch the 2:00 boat, sail for 35 minutes and walk 3 hours back to the car. Now we drive north along the lake, turning left on A5091 and then left again on A66 to Keswick and to your B&B over Newlands.

Sightseeing highlights

● ● **Brockhole National Park Visitors Centre** — This is the place to start your visit to the Lake District. Pick up a copy of 'What's on at Brockhole'. Fine intro slide shows daily at 11:00 and 2:30, info desk, organised walks, special exhibits, bookshop, an excellent cafeteria, gardens, nature walks, large car park. In a big old stately house on the shores of Windermere between Ambleside and the town of Windermere on A591. Open daily 10:00-6:00, £1 entrance fee, tel. (09662) 2231. Our important goal is to arrive here from Blackpool by 11:00 to catch the orientation show. Use the bookshop to buy the Ordnance Survey 'Lake District Tourist Map' (£2.40 ($4)) and a guidebook. I enjoyed the refreshingly opinionated *Good Guide to the Lakes* by Hunter Davies (£2.95 ($5)). Go over your plans (Ullswater ferry schedule) with the info person.

The whole district is dotted with Tourist Information Centres. All are helpful, especially for their specific locality. Use them. Ask for advice.

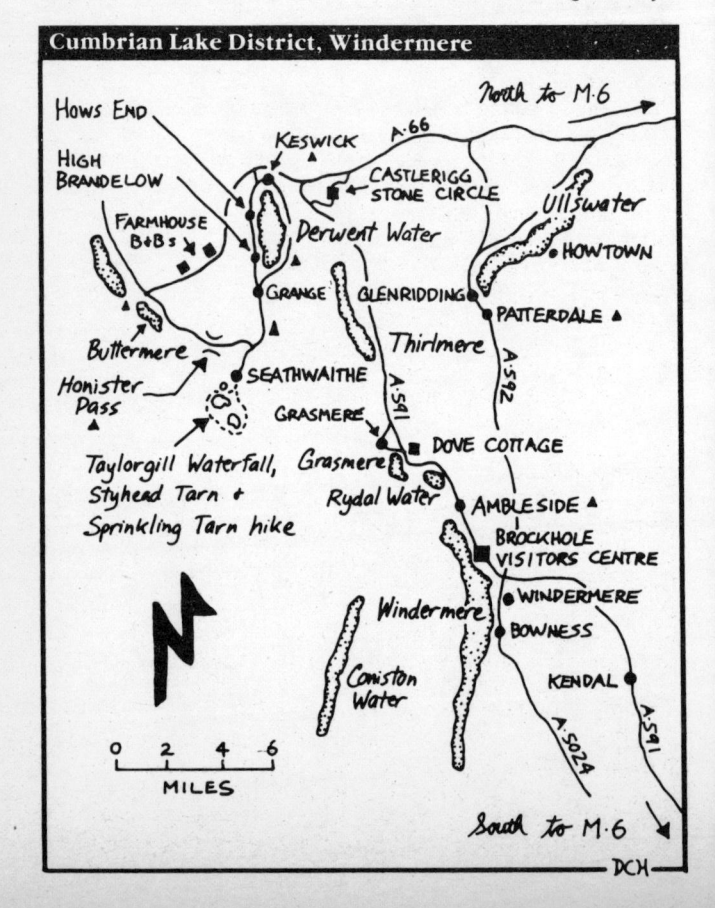

● ● ● **Ullswater hike and boat ride** — Ullswater is considered the most beautiful lake in the area, and this hike is a great way

Cumbrian Lake District, Windermere

Tour 13

to enjoy it. Park your car at the Glenridding dock on the south end of the lake. Be sure to catch the 2:00 boat (it's best to get there 20 minutes early in the summer; 35-minute ride; £1.30 ($2); tel. Glenridding 229 for info) to the first stop, Howtown, halfway up the lake. Then spend three hours hiking and dawdling along the well marked path by the lake south to Patterdale and then along the road back to your car in Glenridding. Good views, varied terrain, a few bridges and farms along the way. I did the walk in tennis shoes in 2½ hours. Bring raingear.

Accommodation

The Lake District abounds with very attractive B&Bs, guest houses and youth hostels. It needs all of them when summer hordes threaten the serenity of this Romantics' mecca. The region is most crowded on Sundays and from mid-July to the beginning of September. Saturdays are not bad. With a car to shop around in, you should have no trouble finding a room, but for a particular place it's best to telephone ahead.

Birkrigg Farm — This is the perfect farmhouse B&B for this trip. Mrs. Margaret Beatty serves visitors with a comfy lounge, evening tea (good for socialising with her other guests), classy breakfast, territorial view, perfect peace and a hot water bottle to warm up your bed (farmhouses lack central heating). She's open late March through to early November, charges £7.50 ($13) and does a fine £4 ($7) dinner for guests who order in advance (a good idea). Her 220-acre farm is shown on the Ordnance Survey map, on the tiny road halfway between Braithwaite (near Keswick) and Buttermere. Birkrigg Farm, Newlands, Keswick, Cumbria, CA12 5TS, tel. (0596) 82278.

Keskadale Farm — Another great farmhouse experience, valley views, super hospitality, £9 ($16), £12 ($21) with dinner. On Newlands Pass Road near a hairpin turn. Call Mrs. Harryman on (Braithwaite) 544.

For village B&Bs try the beautiful valley of Borrowdale (south off Derwent Water). The village of Grange is nice but Rosthwaite is better. **Yew Tree Farm** (Hazel Ralph, tel. (059684) 675) and **Nook Farm** (Carole Jackson, tel. (059684) 677) each charge £4 ($7) and are very old — I mean their houses: saggy floors, thick whitewashed walls, small doorways and hearthocentric (no central heating). If you're interested in farm noises and the old world, these are for you.

Youth Hostels — The Lake District has 30 youth hostels and needs more. Most are great old buildings, handy sources of info, and fun socially. In the summer you'll need to call ahead. For our plan consider the **King George VI Memorial Hostel** — good food, royal setting, ¼ mile south of Buttermere village on Honister Pass road, tel. (059685) 254. Also the **Lougthwaite**

Hostel, secluded in Borrowdale Valley just south of Rosthwaite — well run, drying rooms, tel. (059684) 257. The Derwentwater hostel is especially comfortable while the Patterdale hostel near Ullswater is very friendly. Remember, hostels are marked on most good maps with a red triangle.

Itinerary options
Consider seeing Wordsworth's Dove Cottage today rather than tomorrow. Skip the hike, do the Info Centre and Wordsworth's Dove Cottage. Or, skip breakfast and do Brockhole Centre 10:00-11:30, Dove Cottage 12:00-1:00, and then the hike. Or, skip the Info Centre and do Dove Cottage. Any of these options make tomorrow much easier by doing Wordsworth's place today.

If great scenery is commonplace in your life, the Lake District can be more soothing than exciting. To save time you could easily make this area a one-night stand...or even a quick drive-through.

TOUR 14
EXPLORING THE LAKE DISTRICT

We'll enjoy an easy day today, with a little touring around, choosing from a couple of great Lake District hikes, and visiting the humble house of William Wordsworth, the poet whose appreciation of nature and back-to-basics lifestyle put this area on the map. If you need a holiday from your holiday, use this day to just vegetate and recharge.

Suggested Schedule

9:00 am	Slow breakfast, enjoy your farm.
10:00 am	Explore Buttermere, Honister Pass, Borrowdale.
12:00	Lunch and drive to Grasmere.
1:00 pm	Tour Wordsworth's Dove Cottage and museum.
3:00 pm	Drive to Keswick, see town and catch circular boat (clockwise) to High Brandlehow Pier. Walk along lake to Hawesend Pier. Catch boat to Keswick.
6:00 pm	Drive home (visiting Castlerigg Stone Circle if you have time and energy).

Transport

Nothing is very far from Keswick and Derwentwater. The entire region is just 30 miles by 30 miles. By all means get a good map, get off the big roads and leave the car at least occasionally for some walking. In the summer, the Keswick-Ambleside-Windermere-Bowness area suffers from congestion. Larger lakes are served by old 'steamers', and any T.I. can give you local schedules.

Sightseeing highlights

●●●**Dove Cottage** — Wordsworth spent his most productive years (1799-1808) in this well-preserved old cottage on the edge of Grasmere. Today it is the obligatory sight for any visit to the area. Even if you're not a fan (and I'm not), Wordsworth's style of 'plain living and high thinking', his appreciation of nature and his basic Romanticism are very appealing. The cottage tour is excellent as is the adjoining museum. Even a speedy and jaded museum-goer will want at least an hour here. Open 9:30-5:30, April-September (Sundays from 11:00) and 10:00-4:30 off-season. £2.50 ($4) (£2 ($3.50) with YH card).

Rydal Mount — Wordsworth's final, more high-class home, lovely garden and view. It lacks the charm of Dove Cottage, and is worthwhile only for Wordsworth fans.

● ● **Derwentwater** — One of the region's most beautiful and most popular lakes. With five islands, a good circular boat service, plenty of trails and the pleasant town of Keswick at its north end, the lake entertains. The roadside views aren't much, so walk or cruise. I'd suggest a combined walk/sail trip around the lake and an hour in Keswick (good shops and tourist info). The boats go every 15 minutes in each direction and make seven stops on each 50-minute roundtrip. The best walk is between High Brandlehow and Hawesend. (There's a large car park at the Keswick pier and a small one above Hawesend.)

High Ridge Hike — The best 'king of the mountain' feeling. Park your car at Hawesend, hike up along the ridge to Cat Bells, past the peak to Black Crag and down to High Brandlehow. From there take the easy path along the shore of Derwentwater back to your Hawesend starting point.

● ● **A Waterfall and Two Tarns** — For a rewarding 2 or 3 hour walk park your car south of Borrowdale at the end of a long dead-end road to Seathwaite. Go through the farm, cross the river, continue along the river (it's difficult to follow the trail but keep along the river) and up a steep rocky climb to the Taylor Gill Force — a 140 foot waterfall. There's a hundred yards of rocky scramble here but the trail gets good at the falls. Keep walking to two lovely remote 'tarns' (bodies of water too small to be a lake), circling the Seathwaite Fell to Stockley Bridge and following the bridle path back to your car. For an easy version, just walk to the first tarn and backtrack, eventually taking a right turn leading to Stockley Bridge (get advice at Keswick T.I.).

● ● **Buttermere** — This is the ideal little lake with a lovely mile stroll around it offering nonstop lakeland beauty. If you're not a hiker but wish you were, take this walk. If you're very short on time, at least stop here for a short break. A great road over the rugged Honister Pass connects Buttermere with Borrowdale and Derwentwater.

● ● **Castlerigg Stone Circle** — 38 stones, 90 feet across, 3,000 years old, mysteriously laid out on a line between the two tallest peaks on the horizon. Great setting. Five minutes south of the A66, east of Keswick, well signposted from A66. Look for 'stone circle' exit. Best at sunrise or sunset.

TOUR 15

LAKE DISTRICT TO WEST COAST OF SCOTLAND

Today we drive for six hours to Oban, the gateway to the Hebrides, Scotland's wild and windblown western islands. The last half of the journey is scenic, taking us from big and burly Glasgow along the famous Loch Lomond, deep into the powerful mountains, forests, valleys and lochs of Scotland's west country and to the edge of the Highlands.

Suggested Schedule

9:00 am	Leave Lake District (stopping at the Castlerigg Stone Circle if you haven't yet). Drive 3 hours to Glasgow.
1:00 pm	Stop along Loch Lomond for picnic lunch. Drive on, 3 hours from Glasgow to Oban, enjoying the rugged scenery en route.
4:00 pm	Arrive in Oban, go first to tourist office and then to your B&B.

Transport: drive Lake District to Oban

From Keswick take the A66 to M6 and speed non-stop north, crossing Hadrian's Wall into bonnie Scotland. Here the motorway ends, but the road (A74) stays great, becoming the M74 south of Glasgow. Follow the M74 through Glasgow where it becomes the M8. Cross the Erskine Bridge and head in the direction of Dumbarton via A82. After Dumbarton its the A82, a beautiful (but often congested) lakeside drive along Loch Lomond.

Halfway up the lake, take a left onto A83, drive along saltwater Loch Long and toward Inveraray via Rest-and-be-thankful Pass. (This colourful name comes from the 1880s when 2nd and 3rd class coach passengers got out and *pushed* the 1st class people up the hill! You can bet the 'pushers' and the horses rested and were thankful!)

Inveraray is a lovely castle town on Loch Fyne. Leaving Inveraray, go through a gate (tricky to see) to A819, through Glen Aray and along scenic Loch Awe where you'll meet the A85. Turn left and follow this into Oban.

Glasgow — an Art Nouveau lunch

The flowing organic lines of Art Nouveau, the curvey-for-the-sake-of-curvey turn of the century artistic reaction to the rigid right angles of Industrial Age design, is once again popular.

Scotland

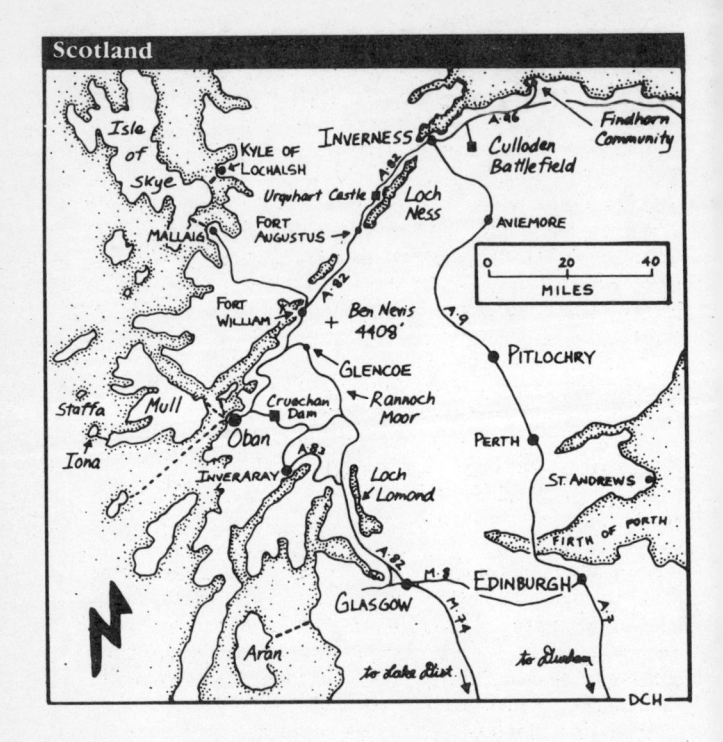

[Map showing Scotland with locations including Isle of Skye, Kyle of Lochalsh, Inverness, Culloden Battlefield, Findhorn Community, Urquhart Castle, Loch Ness, Mallaig, Fort Augustus, Aviemore, Fort William, Ben Nevis 4408', Glencoe, Staffa, Mull, Cruachan Dam, Rannoch Moor, Pitlochry, Iona, Oban, Inveraray, Loch Lomond, Perth, St. Andrews, Firth of Forth, Glasgow, Edinburgh, Aran, with routes to Lake District and Durham. Scale 0-40 miles. Signed DCH.]

Throughout Europe people are on the Jugendstil or Art Nouveau trail.

Charles Mackintosh put Glasgow on the Art Nouveau map and since you're passing through around lunchtime you might consider a short stop. Take exit 18 off the M8 and follow the signs to City Centre. At 217 Sauchiehall Street you'll find Mackintosh's Willow Tea Room serving fine food (£5 ($9) for lunch) in an unforgettable setting. Then walk around George Square, Glasgow's stately and friendly central square, before returning to the M8, crossing the Erskine Bridge and heading into the Highlands.

Art Nouveau fanatics love the Glasgow School of Art. This Mackintosh masterpiece is at 167 Renfrew Street, open Mon-Fri 10:00-12:00 and 2:00-4:00, with tours at 10:30, 11:30, 2:30, and 3:30.

Sightseeing highlights
This 'gateway to the isles' has ferries coming and going all day long. The **Isle of Mull** (3rd largest in Scotland, most scenic, 300 miles of coastline, castle, 3,169-foot-high mountain) is worth

a day. Just beyond it, the historic island of **Iona** (St. Columba brought Christianity here in the 6th century AD; abbey and thousands of visitors) can be visited easily as part of a tour from Oban. A tour beats taking your car on the ferry (too expensive). Get specifics from the excellent T.I. (Open Mon-Fri 9:00-9:00, Sat 9:00-6:00, Sun 3:00-6:00, tel. 63123).

The stark but very green **Island of Kerrera**, just opposite Oban (6 boats a day, 75p, from Gallanach, 2 miles south of Oban), is a quick and easy opportunity to get that romantic island experience. Enjoy a walk, solitude and the sea. The islands of Seil and Luing, a short drive south, are another good sidetrip.

Oban itself has plenty going on in the summer. The T.I. has handouts listing everything from saunas to launderettes to horse riding and what to do in the rain. Use them.

Accommodation

Oban has plenty of B&Bs for its many visitors. The Tourist Info will fill you with details and can find you a room if my suggestions don't work.

Strathlachlan Guest House. This is a winner. Mrs. Rena Anderson charges £9 ($16) for a place that's quiet, clean, stocking-feet cosy, free-and-easy, friendly and chocolate-box tidy. There's a great lounge, easy parking, good central location 2 streets off the water just past Jay's Tearoom. 2 Strathaven Terrace, Oban, Argyll, tel. 0631-63861.

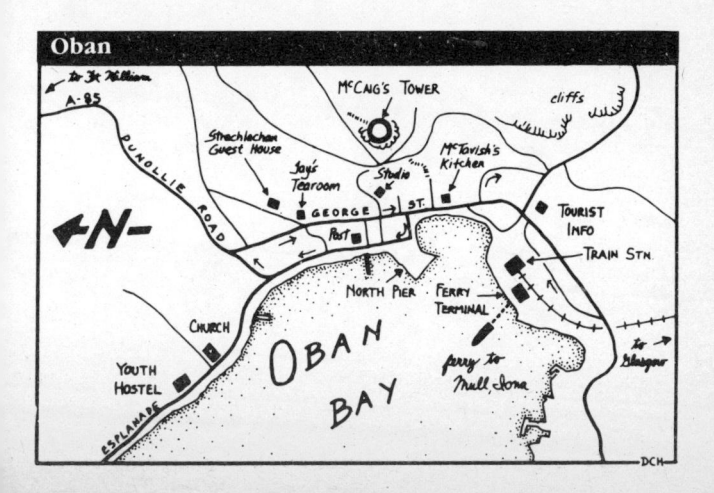

Achanmara Hotel — On the 'Esplanade' seafront promenade. A lovely location with an island view, 3 minutes from the town centre. This is a grand old hotel with hotel-style formality, but charging a reasonable £10 ($17), tel. 62683.

Rahoy Lodge — On Gallanach Road about a mile south of town, overlooking the beach and islands. A bit eccentric — a 'lived in' lodge. £8.50 ($15), tel. (0631) 62301.

Youth Hostel, on the 'Esplanade', alongside the finest hotels in town, in a grand building with a grand piano, and a harbour/island view. £3 ($5), tel. 62025. Open only April-October.

Food

Oban has plenty of eating options. In season, try to mix dinner and some Scottish folk entertainment. **McTavish's Kitchen** on the central George Street is a plain-looking cafeteria which serves hearty cheap food and live folk music and dance on most nights. **Jay's Tearoom** nearby is a comfy place with an interesting menu for a light meal.

The **Studio** on Craigard Road has a real hit-the-spot-on-a-stormy-day stew. The **Oban Inn** is a fun local pub.

Tour 16

TOUR 16
HIGHLANDS, LOCH NESS, SCENIC DRIVE

Today is mostly driving — but joy-riding — with a chance to see the harsh Highland beauty of Glencoe, the engineering beauty of the Caledonian Canal, and the soft beauty of Loch Ness — which is worth a look even if you don't see the monster. How far you get today depends on the weather, the traffic and your eagerness to get to bonnie Edinburgh.

Suggested Schedule

9:00 am	Leave Oban.
10:00 am	Explore Glencoe.
11:00 am	Drive Glencoe to Fort Augustus.
12:00	Loch Ness, castle, picnic, monster business.
3:00 pm	Culloden Battlefield.
4:00 pm	Drive south.
7:00 pm	Possibly set up in Edinburgh.

Transport
Scotland's roads have improved remarkably in the last few years. You'll make great time on good, mostly two-lane roads today unless traffic gets in the way. Don't be timid about passing. Study the locals. If you don't overtake, diesel fumes and large trucks may be your memory of 'Tour 16'.

From Oban, follow the coastal A828 noticing the enchanting ruined island castle on your left a few minutes north of town. At Loch Leven go in to Glencoe. Skip the town and drive 10 miles inland until you hit the vast, depressingly flat Rannoch Moor. Then make a U-turn and return through the valley. Continue north over the bridge, past boring Fort William and on towards Loch Ness. For 60 miles you'll follow the Caledonian Canal and A82 to Inverness. Follow signs to A9 (south to Perth) and just as you leave Inverness (not worth a stop) turn east off A9 onto B9006 to the Culloden Battlefield Visitors Centre. Back on A9 it's a wonderfully speedy and very scenic road (A9, M90, A90) all the way to Edinburgh. If traffic is light, you can drive from Inverness to Edinburgh in 2½ hours.

Sightseeing highlights
● ● **Glencoe** — This is the essence of the wild, powerful and stark beauty of the Highlands (and I think excuses the hurried tourist from needing to go north of Inverness). Along with its

scenery, Glencoe offers a good dose of bloody clan history. Stop in at the visitors centre to learn about the 'murder under trust' of 1692, when the Campbells massacred the sleeping MacDonalds and the valley got its nickname, 'The Weeping Glen'.

Ben Nevis — At Fort William you'll pass Ben Nevis, Britain's highest peak (over 4,400 feet). Thousands of visitors walk to its summit each year but we'll just hope for a clear day and admire her from the car.

● **Caledonian Canal** — Scotland is sliced in half by three lochs (Oich, Lochy, and Ness) connected in the early 1800s with a series of canals and locks by the great engineer, Telford. As you drive the 60 miles from Ft. William to Inverness follow Telford's work — 40 miles of lakes, 20 miles of canals, locks, raising ships from sea level to 51 feet (Ness) to 93 feet (Lochy) to 106 feet (Oich). Fort Augustus is the best stop. Drop into its free museum for more information.

● **Loch Ness** — I'll admit, I had my eyes on the water. The local tourist industry thrives on the legend of the Loch Ness monster. It's a thrilling thought, and there have been several seemingly reliable 'sightings' (priests, policemen, and now sonar images) but I didn't buy it. The Loch Ness Monster Info Centre (open 9:00 am-9:30 pm daily, £1.65 ($3), in Drumnadrochit) is tacky and a disappointment; if you've got half an hour and a couple of pounds to blow, see if I'm right. The nearby Urquhart Castle ruins (Mon-Fri 9:30-7:00, Sat-Sun 2:00-7:00, £1) are gloriously situated with a view of virtually the entire Loch Ness and make for a better stop than the monster centre. Drumnadrochit has its Highland Games on the last Saturday of each August.

● **Culloden Battlefield** — Bonnie Prince Charlie was defeated here in 1746. This last battle fought on British soil spelled the end of the Jacobite resistance and the fall of the clans. The visitors centre makes the short detour worthwhile with a great AV show, a furnished old cottage, the memorial and other exhibits. (Daily 9:30-8:00.)

Findhorn Foundation — This international spiritual community, famous for its sensitivity to nature and its tremendously green thumb, greets visitors with 2:00 tours Mon, Wed & Sat. 20 miles east of Inverness, drive through Forres and follow signs to Findhorn.

Scottish words
aye — yes
ben — mountain
bonnie — beautiful
carn, **cairn** — heap of stones
creag, **crag** — rock, cliff
haggis — rich meat dish (bladder stuffed with sheep's offal).

inch, innis — island
inver — river, mouth
kyle — strait, firth
loch — lake
neeps — turnips
tattie — potato

Accommodation
Here's where things get murky. You can get to Edinburgh if you really push. You'll arrive late, so be sure to have a firm hold on a bed and call at 5:00 with your ETA (see Edinburgh Accommodation below).

A more relaxed plan is to find a room somewhere between Culloden and Pitlochry. Inverness has plenty of rooms — but not much reason to stop. I'd head south to find a place in one of many pleasant towns along the A9. Pitlochry is a lovely mountain town. Its tourist office (open till 8:30, tel. 0796-2215) can find you a room. The **youth hostel** on Knockard Road on a hill above the main street (£3.50 ($6), tel. 0796-2308) is excellent. Also consider the **Craigroyston House**, right in the centre, or **Mrs. Maxwell's B&B** on Lower Oakfield Street (tel. 0796-2053).

TOUR 17
EDINBURGH

Edinburgh is Scotland's showpiece — historical, monumental, entertaining, well-organised — it's a tourist delight and I think one of Europe's greatest cities. We'll have nearly two days here — and we'll need every minute.

Suggested Schedule

9:00 am	Drive into Edinburgh from the Highlands.
12:00	Arrive in Edinburgh, park in central railway station car park, do your tourist information chores, have lunch in the Waverley Centre downstairs, or picnic in the Princes Street Gardens. Call B&B to say you're in town. Browse through Waverley Centre and the Princes Gardens.
2:00 pm	Climb Scott Monument for orientation view. Understand town lay-out: Royal Mile on ridge from castle to palace, former Nor Loch lake bed, New Georgian town.
2:30 pm	Georgian walk — down Rose Street, up Castle Street, left down George Street to Charlotte Square. Tour the Georgian House at No. 7. Don't miss its video.
5:00 pm	Return to car, drive to B&B, check in.

Option: if you arrived the night before, it would be best to visit the tourist office that night or first thing in the morning, and switch tours 17 and 18, doing the castle and Royal Mile first, and the Georgian town with free time on the second day in Edinburgh.

Transport

You'll be arriving in the evening of one day or about noon on the next day, depending on which you favour — the country thrills of the Highlands or the city thrills of Edinburgh. Either way, follow the signs to city centre and the centre's intersection of Princes Street and Waverley Bridge.

Arriving in the evening: Park wherever you can and run into the tourist info office (open till 9:00 in July and August) before driving to your B&B.

Mid-day: Turn on to Waverley Bridge, then left into the railway station, park in the huge central car park and climb past the

Tour 17

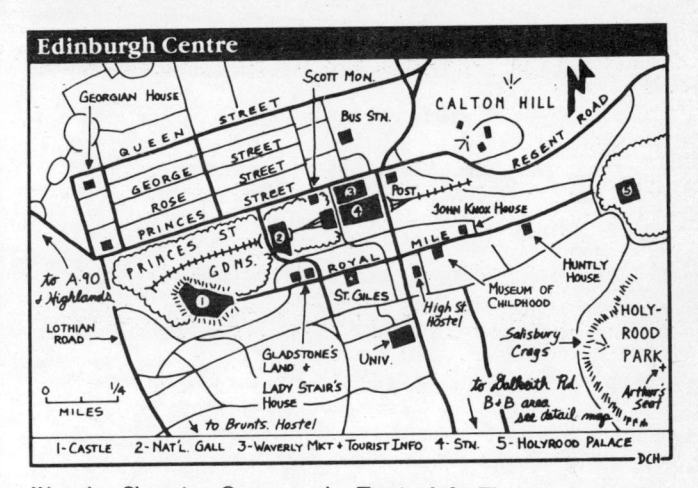

Edinburgh Centre

1-CASTLE 2-NAT'L. GALL 3-WAVERLY MKT + TOURIST INFO 4-STN. 5-HOLYROOD PALACE

Waverley Shopping Centre to the Tourist Info. That evening, drive to your B&B (Call your B&B upon arrival to explain your plans.)

You won't need your car again until you leave Edinburgh. City buses (routes listed in basic 20p city map at T.I; average fare 20 to 30p) and taxis (easy to flag down, several handy pick up points, 70p drop charge, average trip between city centre and the B&B district — £1.50 ($2.50)) are easy and inexpensive while parking and traffic are a real headache. Within town nearly all sights are within walking distance.

Orientation

Edinburgh is two basic towns divided by what was once a lake. The lake (Nor Loch) was drained and is now a lovely park and community centre containing the helpful tourist information centre, Waverley Shopping Centre, the railway station and car park, the starting point for most city bus tours, the festival office, and National Gallery.

The old town was actually a volcanic ridge running south of the lake. This became packed with historic and fascinating buildings bounded on the summit by the great castle and on the bottom by the Holyrood Palace. This is the 'Royal Mile' which, in its day, was called the most crowded city in the world. Houses, shops and arcades were narrow and tall with 'closes', or little courtyards, connected to 'High Street' by narrow lanes or even tunnels. This colourful jumble is the tourist's Edinburgh.

To alleviate crowding, the lake was drained and a magnificent Georgian city, today's 'New Town', was laid out to the north. Georgian Edinburgh, like Bath, shone with broad boulevards, straight streets, square squares, circular circuses, and elegant mansions decked out in colonnades, pediments, and sphinxes all in the proud style of 200 years ago.

Sightseeing highlights

Be organised with this list of sights to get the most out of your two days in Edinburgh. Your first stop on arrival must be the Tourist Information Centre in its new location, central as can be atop the Waverley Centre on Princes Street. Open 8:30-9:00 in July and August, 8:30-8:00 in June and September, and 9:00-6:00 off season, Sundays only from 11:00, Tel. (031) 557-2727).

Buy a city map (20p) and city 'Official Guide Book' (£1.50 ($2.50)) and 'Edinburgh, a Guide to the Royal City' (85p), and pick up 'What's On' and 'Walking Tours in the City Centre' brochures. Confirm your sightseeing plans and hours as described below, and ask about walking tours down the Royal Mile, evening events and entertainment, and mid-day concerts in the park.

- **Walter Scott Monument** — An elaborate neo-Gothic building (like Albert Memorial and Houses of Parliament in London) honouring the great author, one of Edinburgh's many illustrious sons. (Built 1844, 200 feet high, 287 steps to a fine city orientation view.)
- **Rose Street** — The New (or Georgian) Town's most interesting street. Pedestrians only, interesting shops, and 21 pubs. A pleasant stroll by day and quite a crawl after dark.
- • **Georgian Edinburgh** — The grand George Street connects St. Andrews and Charlotte Squares. This is the centrepiece of the elegantly planned New Town. Don't miss the refurbished Georgian House at No. 7 Charlotte Square with an interesting video introduction and a lady in each lavish room bursting with stories and trivia. Open Mon-Sat 10:00-5:00, Sunday 2:00-5:00.

Accommodation

Edinburgh, the festival city, is packed in the summer. But it has lots of B&Bs, hotels and hostels with a super tourist office to make the needed connections.

The annual festival fills the city every year from the beginning of August until about September 8. Conventions, school holidays and other surprises can make room-finding tough at almost any time. Phone ahead, use the Tourist Office or at least arrive early.

The best B&B district is, without a doubt, south of town. You'll find street after street of B&Bs south of the Royal Commonwealth Pool between Orange Road and Dalkeith Road. This area is a twenty-minute walk from the Royal Mile, well served by city buses, comfortably safe and loaded with eateries, launderettes, shops, etc.

Tour 17   85

Edinburgh: Our Neighbourhood

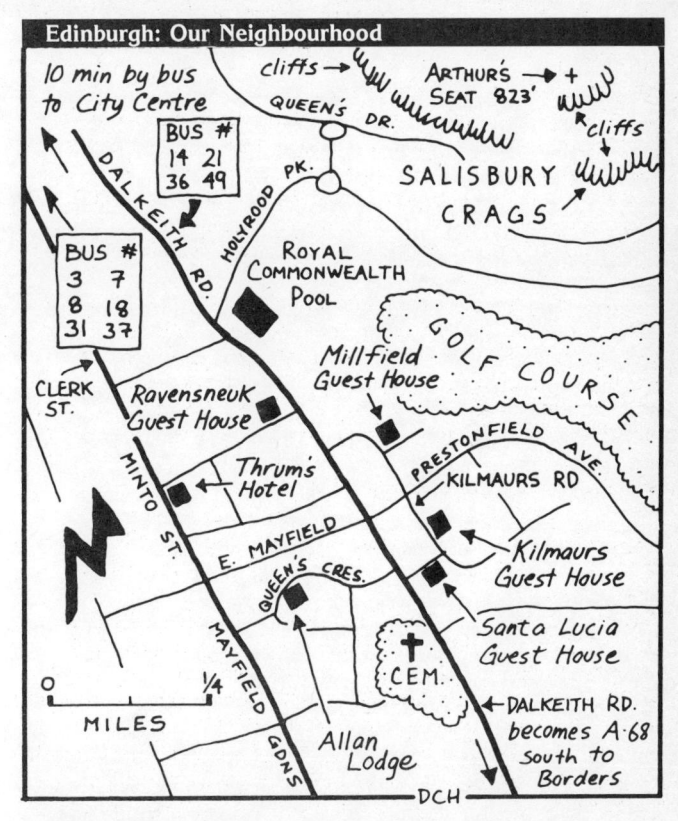

[Map showing the neighborhood with the following labels: 10 min by bus to City Centre; Cliffs; Arthur's Seat 823'; Queen's Dr.; Bus # 14, 21, 36, 49; Dalkeith Rd.; Holyrood Pk.; Cliffs; Salisbury Crags; Bus # 3, 7, 8, 18, 31, 37; Royal Commonwealth Pool; Clerk St.; Ravensneuk Guest House; Millfield Guest House; Golf Course; Thrum's Hotel; Prestonfield Ave.; Kilmaurs Rd.; Minto St.; E. Mayfield; Kilmaurs Guest House; Queen's Cres.; Mayfield Gdns.; Cem.; Santa Lucia Guest House; Allan Lodge; Dalkeith Rd. becomes A-68 south to Borders; 0 – ¼ Miles; DCH]

Millfield Guest House — Mrs. Liz Broomfield's place is great with an entertaining proprietor, quiet street, and easy parking, and bus stop around the corner; comfy TV lounge, good phone for long distance calls. £10 ($17), tel. (031) 667-4428, at 12 Marchhall Road (just east off Dalkeith Road, south of pool).

Kilmaurs Guest House — Just down the street from the Millfield Guest House, Mr. and Mrs. Christie make you feel right at home — clean, TV in room, £10 ($17), at 9 Kilmaur Road, tel. (031) 667-8315.

Ravensneuk Guest House is nearby at 11 Blacket Avenue, tel. (031) 667-5347, across Dalkeith Road. At £10.50 ($18), it's a good third choice.

These B&Bs (and many more nearby) are well served by buses. On Dalkeith Road, Nos. 14, 21, 36 and 49 (all but No. 2) take you into town. On Minto Street Nos. 3, 7, 8, 18, 31 & 37 do the same. The handy launderette at 208 Dalkeith Road is open

Mon-Fri 8:30-5:00, Sat-Sun 10:00-2:00. Wonderful take-away Chinese food on Minto Street, and handy cafeteria overlooking huge Commonwealth Pool.

Thrum's Private Hotel — This small hotel offers rooms with private bathrooms, £12.50 ($22) single, £25 ($44) double. Mr. & Mrs. Mahoney, tel. 667-5545, at 14 Minto Street.

Allan Lodge Guest House — Delightful location on a quiet crescent between Dalkeith Road and Minto Street. Mrs. Nichol charges £10-12 ($17-21) per person, including free access to a private park behind the house. 37 Queen's Crescent, tel. 668-2947.

Santa Lucia Guest House — Friendly accommodation by effervescent Mrs. Laird, £11 ($19), 14 Kilmaurs Terrace, tel. 667-8694.

Youth Hostels — The T.I. has a list of cheap beds. The best hostel in town is the **Bruntsfield Hostel**, on a park, at No. 7 Bruntsfield Crescent. Well-run, £3 ($5), buses Nos. 11, 15, 16 to and from Princes Street, tel. 447-2994. The other YHA hostel at 17 Eglinton Crescent is also good (337-1120). The YWCAs at 226-3842, 225-3608 and 229-4850 are for women only, open all year. The tourist office has a list of more cheap beds.

Recently opened in Edinburgh is the **High Street Independent Hostel**. Just your basic hostel bed, but a smashing location just off the Royal Mile! Open all day (7:00 am to 1:30 am), five minutes from the railway station, kitchen, sporadic showers, nightly films and a friendly atmosphere. £4 ($7), no breakfast. 8 Blackfriars Street, tel. 557-3984.

Food

Restaurants are good, plentiful, and rather expensive. For cheap eating, go ethnic — especially Chinese take away and pub lunches (Scottish pubs don't serve evening meals). Or try the **Commonwealth Pool** cafeteria, or the **Waverley Centre Food Circus**, a ring of flashy trendy fast food joints offering a plastic galaxy of choices. At Waverley try **McTavishes** for hearty, inexpensive, traditional Scottish specialities like haggis. Or picnic. The T.I. has brochures and books on dining locally.

TOUR 18
EDINBURGH

Today, we'll continue our look at Edinburgh, visiting the castle, exploring our way down the history-packed Royal Mile to the Holyrood Palace. Our Scottish finale will be an evening of folk fun, food and music.

Suggested Schedule

9:00 am	Breakfast and bus to High Street or taxi to Castle Esplanade.
9:30 am	Tour Castle
11:00 am	Do Royal Mile: Gladstone Land, Lady Stair's House, pub lunch, St. Giles Cathedral, Knox's House, Huntly House, Craft Centre.
4:00 pm	Tour Holyrood Palace.
7:00 pm	Scottish Evening — dinner show in hotel or simple dinner and folk music in a pub.

Sightseeing highlights along the Royal Mile

● ● ● **Royal Mile** — One of Europe's most interesting historic walks, whether you follow a local guide (daily, free, during the summer) or do-it-yourself with a Royal Mile guidebook. Each step of the way is entertaining. Start at the top and loiter your way downhill to the palace. Below are the top sights of the Royal Mile — working downhill.

● ● **Edinburgh Castle** — The fortified birthplace of the city 1,300 years ago, this is the imposing symbol of Edinburgh. Start with the free 20-minute guided intro tour, leaving every few minutes from inside the gate. Don't miss the Scottish National War Memorial, Banqueting Hall with fine Scottish Crown Jewels, the room full of Battle of Culloden mementos, St. Margaret's Chapel (oldest building in town), the giant cannon and the city view from the ramparts (best seen in that order). Allow 90 minutes including the tour. Open Mon-Sat 9:30-5:30, Sunday 11:00-5:30. Entrance fee £2 ($3.50).

● ● **Gladstone's Land** — Your best look at a typical 16th-17th century house with lived-in furnished interior and guides in each room. The best Royal Mile photo is from from the top floor window. Open Mon-Sat 10:00-5:00, Sunday 2:00-5:00.

● **Lady Stair's House** — An interesting house from 1622 filled with manuscripts and knick-knacks of Scotland's three greatest literary figures, Robert Burns, Sir Walter Scott and Robert Louis Stevenson. Interesting for anyone, fantastic for fans. Open 10:00-6:00, closed Sundays.

St. Giles Cathedral — Interesting Gothic church, don't miss the ornate, medieval thistle chapel or the Scottish crown steeple.

John Knox's House — Fascinating if you're into Reformation history. This fine 16th century house is filled with things from the life of the Great Reformer. Mon-Sat 10:00-5:00, closed Sundays.

Huntly House — Another old house full of old stuff. It's free and worth a look for its early Edinburgh history. Don't miss the copy of the National Covenant written on an animal skin, and the sketches of pre-Georgian Edinburgh with its lake still wet. Open 10:00-6:00, closed Sundays.

Crafts Centre in the Acheson House (in courtyard next to Huntly House) — Full of entertaining network by 300 local crafts people. Free.

● **Holyrood Palace** — This bottom end of the Royal Mile is the Queen's residence when she's in town. Guided tours only of the royal apartments, state apartment, and lots of rich furnishings, paintings and history. Open Mon-Sat 9:30-6:00, Sunday 10:30-5:15 (closed when in use).

Other Edinburgh sightseeing highlights

● **Arthur's Seat** — The 823-foot volcanic mountain surrounded by a fine park overlooking Edinburgh. A 30-minute walk up from the Holyrood Palace or from the Commonwealth Pool, with a rewarding view. The easiest 'I climbed a mountain' feeling I've ever had.

Princes Street Gardens — This grassy former lake bed separates Edinburgh's new and old towns with a wonderful escape from the citiness of it all. Plenty of free concerts and dancing in the summer and the oldest floral clock in the world. Join local office workers in a picnic lunch break.

National Gallery — An elegant neo-Classical building with a small but impressive collection of European masterpieces and the best look you'll get at Scottish paintings. Mon-Sat 10:00-5:00, Sunday 2:00-5:00.

Royal Commonwealth Games Swimming Pool — The biggest pool I've ever seen. Open to the public, swim-suit and towel hire, good cafeteria, weights, saunas, etc.

City bus tours — Edinburgh offers a stunning array of tours taking you around the city or around Scotland. The half-day tours of greater Edinburgh take over where your feet leave off. One-day tours can take you as far as the Western Islands, Oban, and Loch Ness. Tours leave from the Mound, near the railway station.

Greyhound Races — If you've never seen dog racing, this is a fun night out offering great people-watching, and a chance to lose some money gambling. About two nights a week at

Powderhall Stadium (see 'What's On' schedule).
Edinburgh Crystal — Blowing, moulding, cutting, polishing, engraving. The Edinburgh Crystal Company gives by far the best glass works tour I've seen (puts Venice to shame). 10 miles south of town (A701) in Penicuik. 45-minute tours leave regularly from 9:00-3:30 (75p, except free from 9:00-10:00). There's a shop full of 'bargain' second quality pieces, video show, good cafeteria. Consider half-day tours from the Mound or doing it on your way south. Phone first, (0968) 75128, and try to avoid the 11:15-12:45 factory lunch break.
Stirling Castle — Skip it. It's very famous, but is currently used as a barracks — a disappointment. The town is pleasantly medieval, however, and many commute (one hour by train) to the more hectic Edinburgh from there.
● ● ● **The Edinburgh Festival** — August and September — One of *the* events of Europe, the annual festival turns Edinburgh into a carnival of culture. There's enough music, dance, art and drama to make even the most jaded tourist drool with excitement. Every day is jammed with formal and spontaneous fun.

The festival rages from mid-August through to September's first week with the 'fringe festival' and the Military Tattoo starting a few days early. Many city sights run on extended hours and those that normally close on Sundays don't. Local students give free Royal Mile walking tours, and all in all it's a glorious time to be in Edinburgh.

Major events sell out well in advance, but every day is packed with top-notch 'ticket at the door' opportunities. Look into tickets from London at the start of your tour and do whatever you can to get a ticket to the massed bands, drums, bagpipes and sometimes even elephants of the Military Tattoo (nightly except Thursday and Sunday, at the Castle, tel. 225-1188 for info). Keep in mind that the equally wonderful and more informal Fringe Festival (tel. 226-5257) has literally hundreds of events that only sell tickets at the door. Your major festival worry is getting a room. After that get a programme — and you're all set for a cultural extravaganza. If you do manage to hit the festival, be sure to add at least a third day here.
Shopping — The best shopping is along Princes Street (don't miss elegant old Jenner's Department Store), the mod and flashy Waverley Centre, Rose Street and the Royal Mile.
Hours — 9:00-5:30, staying open late on Thurdsays.
● ● **Folk Music** — Edinburgh offers either folk music in pubs or more organised 'Scottish folk evenings', generally in more expensive hotels. For from £10 to £20 ($17 to $35) at several hotels on nearly any night you can enjoy a traditional — or at least what the tourists believe is traditional — meal with the full

slate of swirling kilts, blaring bagpipes and colourful Scottish folk dancing. Plenty of details at T.I. or in 'What's On'.

For a basic informal evening of folk music, find the right pub. My favourite Scottish band, the 'North Sea Gas', plays every Friday, 8:30-11:00, free, at Platform One in the Caledonian Hotel on Princes Street. Pubs that feature folk music almost nightly are the White Hart (Grassmarket), Fables (West Port), Royal Oak (Infirmary Street) and the Waverley Bar (St. Mary Street). 'What's On' lists current folk music spots, and nearly any cabbie knows a hot spot or can find one by asking on his radio. (In general, cabbies are a great ace-in-the-hole source of information.)

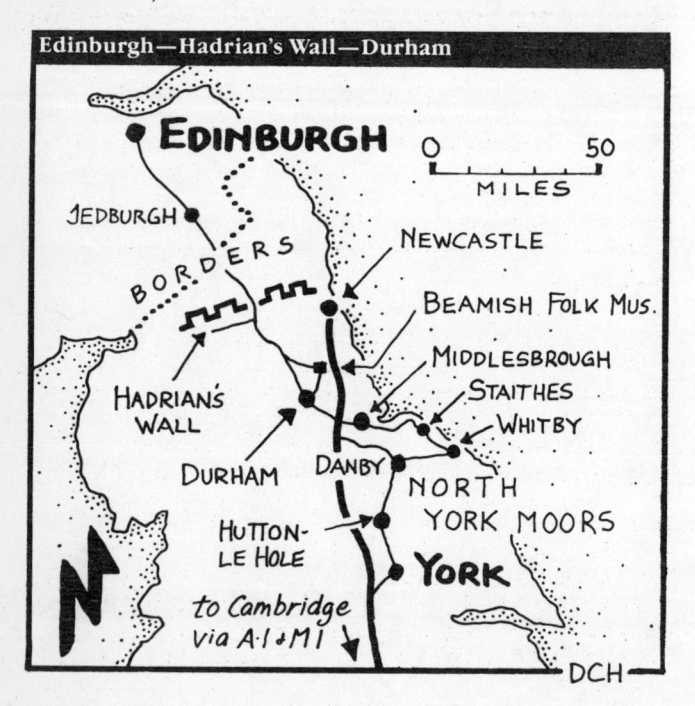

TOUR 19
EDINBURGH – HADRIAN'S WALL – DURHAM

From Edinburgh we head south, filling today with fascinating sights from the years 100, 1200 and 1900 AD. We'll visit Hadrian's Wall, ancient Rome's northernmost boundary, marvel at Durham Cathedral, England's greatest Normal building, and relive the dawn of our century at the great Beamish folk Museum.

Suggested Schedule	
8:30 am	Leave Edinburgh.
11:00 am	Arrive at Hadrian's Wall, tour fort, museum, take a walk along wall, lunch.
1:00 pm	Drive to Beamish Museum
2:00 pm	Beamish Open Air Museum.
5:00 pm	Drive to Durham.
5:30 pm	Arrive Durham, visit T.I., get B&B, tour cathedral.

Transport

From Edinburgh, Dalkeith Road leads south, becoming the A68. (There's a handy supermarket on the left just as you leave Dalkeith Town, ten minutes south of Edinburgh, parking behind.) A68 takes you all the way to Hadrian's Wall in 2½ hours. You'll pass Jedburgh and its abbey after one hour. (There's a tour bus delight just before Jedburgh with kilt makers, woollens, and a sheepskin shop. In Jedburgh, across from a lovely abbey, is a good visitors centre and public toilets.) The England/Scotland border (great view and 'Mr. Softy' ice cream and tea caravan) is a fun quick stop. Before Hexham, roller-coaster down the A6079 two miles to B6318. This great little road follows the Roman Wall westward. Notice the Wall with its trenches on either side as you go. After ten minutes and several 'severe dips', pull into the Housestead's Roman Fort information centre. The Roman fort is on the right.

After your visit, take the small road past Vindolanda (another Roman fort and museum) to the A69. Go east past Hexham, then south on the A68. After a few miles turn east on B6278 through lovely little Snods Edge, through Blackhill to Stanley. The Beamish Museum is well signposted between Stanley and Chester-le-Street.

After the museum follow the signs west past Chester-le-Street to the Motorway. Head south. Just before you enter Durham's old town centre (Cathedral and castle) turn left into the modern

multi-storey car park. (Parking in old Durham is miserable.)
From the 7th floor a walkway takes you right into the old town.

The route from Durham south to the North York Moors is tricky. Whatever you do, don't get sucked into the Stockton-Middlesborough mess. Take the Motorway all the way to Darlington before heading east along the A67.

Sightseeing highlights
● ● ● **Hadrian's Wall** — One of England's most thought-provoking sights. The Romans built this great stone wall during the reign of the Emperor Hadrian (around 130 AD) to protect England from invading Scottish tribes. It stretches 74 miles from coast to coast. Defended by nearly 10,000 troops with fortlets every mile, it was flanked by ditches 15 feet deep. Today several chunks of the wall, ruined forts and museums attract visitors.

By far the best single stop is the Housesteads Fort with a fine museum, national park info centre (with car park and snack bar), and the best preserved segment of the wall surrounded by powerful scenery (open daily 10:00-6:00). From Housesteads, walk west along the Wall. Vindolanda, a larger Roman fort and museum, is just south of the wall and worth a visit only if you devoured the Housesteads museum and are still hungry.

● ● ● **Beamish Open Air Museum** — A huge and unique centre that energetically takes its visitors back to turn-of-the-century Northumbria. You'll need three hours to explore the 1900 town, railway station, mining camp and working farm. This isn't wax, its real. Attendants at each stop explain everything, a video show orientates you and an old tramway saves the wear and tear on your feet. Open 10:00-6:00 daily, well worth £2.50 ($4.50). This is the only museum I've seen covering the dawn of our century.

● ● **Durham Cathedral** — This is the best — and least altered — Norman Cathedral in England and the only one in this itinerary. Study the difference between this heavy Romanesque fortress of worship and the light-filled Gothic of later centuries. Pick up the 10p guide, climb the 300 steps and pay the 50 pence for a great view from the tower. There's also a good cafeteria. Open 7:15 am-8:00 pm daily, until 5:00 pm September May, 5:15 evensong services.

The old town of Durham cuddles the cathedral, surrounded on 3 sides by its river. It has a medieval cobbled atmosphere and an interesting market just off the main square, but still is exciting only for its cathedral.

Accommodation — it's your option:

Durham — This is the easiest plan, stopping early and not having to rush the day. You'll be cutting the North York Moors short to spend the evening in the pleasant medieval city of Durham. Phone ahead or visit the tourist info upon arrival, before visiting the cathedral. (T.I. open Monday-Friday 9:00-6:00, Saturday 9:00-5:00, Sunday 2:00-5:00, tel. 43720, leaves list of vacancies on door after hours.)

Most B&Bs are clustered west of the town centre in Hawthorn Terrace, Crossgate, The Avenue and Sutton Street. Since this is a historical area, B&B signs aren't allowed. Your best bet is to ask at a neighbourhood pub. The **City Hotel** near the river (tel. 69936) has £24 ($42) doubles. The **Durham Castle** is a student residence that rents its 100 singles and 30 doubles to travellers from mid-July through September (B&B for £10 ($17), tel. 0385-65481). A fine B&B is the **Castleview Guest House**, located at 4 Crossgate just over the bridge near the town square. Mike and Anne Williams charge £12 ($21) per person.

For dinner the **House of Andrews** (at 73 Saddler Street in the old town) and the **Traveller's Rest** pub (in Clay Path Street behind the T.I.) are both good.

Staithes — Famous as Captain Cook's boyhood town, this is a salty tumble of cottages bunny-hopping down a ravine and into a tiny harbour. Fishermen still outnumber tourists in undiscovered Staithes.

The Harbourside Guest House, right on the seafront, provides a basic bed, good meals (try the lobster) and the sound of waves to lull you to sleep. Owner Jeff Walker serves up what he claims is 'the best breakfast in Yorkshire'. £10 ($17), tel. 0947-840577.

If he's full, Staithes has several B&Bs. **Kirkhill House**, in Church Street up from Cook's house, has nice rooms at a bargain £7.50 ($13) price. Call Rose Estill on 841058.

Note: Getting to Staithes is no picnic. You'll have to brave the messy Middlesborough motorway maze and head south on the A173 towards Whitby until you see a sign for Staithes on your left.

Whitby — A fun resort town full of amusements. Lots of B&Bs, a great abbey, people scene. Visiting here will rush your day, but if you want a mini-Blackpool, go for it. Like Staithes, just a short journey from the Moors.

On the north edge of the North York Moors — To get an early start in the Moors, leave Durham by 6:00 and find a place somewhere between Guisborough, Danby and Goathland. There are plenty of good B&Bs in the romantic Moors.

TOUR 20
NORTH YORK MOORS AND YORK

Today, we'll drive through the harsh heart of the North York Moors for a good dose of its special stark beauty. Then we'll set up and orientate ourselves in York, one of England's most exciting cities.

Suggested Schedule

8:30 am	Leave your Durham B&B at 8:00 (or 9:30 if you're already in Moor country).
10:00 am	Danby Lodge — North York Moors Visitors Centre Tour exhibition, pick up map, get help with Moors plan.
11:00 am	Drive over Moors, short stop at Hetton le Hole.
12:00	Drive to York.
1:00 pm	Arrive York, check into B&B, park car for good, visit Tourist Info, lunch in King's Manor.
2:15 pm	Walking tour of city (at 7:00 pm in summer)
4:30 pm	Railway Museum or free in old town.

Sightseeing highlights

● **Danby Lodge** — North York Moors Visitors Centre, ideal for your moors orientation. It's a grand old lodge offering exhibits, special shows and nature walks, an info desk with plenty of books and maps, brass rubbing, a cafeteria, and brochures on several good walks that start right there. Open daily 10:00-5:00.

● **North Yorkshire Moors Railway** — If you're tired of driving (or without wheels), this 18-mile, 50-minute steam engine ride from Grosmont and Goathland to Pickering goes through some of the best parts of the moor almost hourly. For info call (0751) 72508. For taped schedule info — 73535. Pickering is worth a stopover — rural life museum, castle, and a market on Mondays.

● **Hetton le Hole** — Postcard-pretty town with the fine little Ryedale Museum, showing 'farmlife in the moors' — reconstructed and furnished 18th century local buildings. Use the nearby car park and the public toilets. Open daily 11:00-6:00, April-October.

Castle Howard — Especially popular now since the filming of *Brideshead Revisited*, this is a fine palatial home, but Blenheim's better.

Rievaulx Abbey — A highlight of the North York Moors but a rerun of fine old abbeys we've already seen.

Tour 20

York

York is a walker's delight but a driver's purgatory. Don't even think of taking the car through the old city gates. Park near Bootham Street. All sights are within walking distance, and if you like you can pay £1.50 ($3) for an all day pass on the yellow bus circuit that goes around and around constantly, connecting the major sights (with commentary, pick up leaflet at T.I.).

Sightseeing highlights — York

Tourist Information — Your first stop. Pick up official guidebook (75p includes map) and 'What's On' and confirm plans. Open Monday-Saturday, 9:00-8:00, Sunday 2:00-5:00. October-May, Monday-Saturday 9:00-5:00, closed Sunday. Tel. 21756. Walk here after parking near Bootham Street.

● ● **Walking Tours** — Voluntary local guides give free two hour walks through York daily at 10:15 and 2:15 from April through to October (plus 7:00 pm in July and August). These meet next to Bootham Bar across from the T.I. in Exhibition Square. An ideal orientation.

There are many other York walking tours. The popular ghost tours go nightly and are the best of their kind in England.

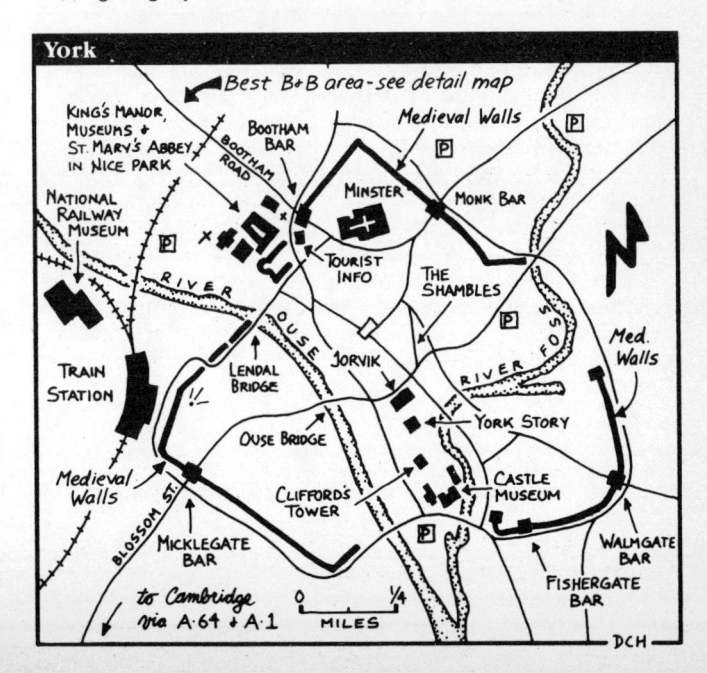

● **City Walls** — The historic walls of York provide a fine 2½ mile walk. Be sure to walk from Bootham Bar (gate) to Monk Bar for outstanding cathedral views. Open till dusk, free.

● **Railway Museum** — A huge national museum showing 150 fascinating years of British Railway history. Two round-houses of historic carriages and engines including Queen Victoria's lavish royal carriage, the very first 'stagecoaches on rails', plus video shows and much more. This is the best railway museum anywhere. Very popular, free, 10-minute walk from centre, open Monday-Saturday 10:00-6:00, Sunday 2:30-6:00.

Accommodation

York has plenty of beds and, since we'll be pulling in at noon, finding a room shouldn't be too tough. The tourist office has an efficient room-finding service (tel. 21756, open 9:00-8:00). There are several student-type hostels (listed in *Let's Go* or at the T.I.). The best B&B district is just five or ten minutes from the Minster past the T.I. up Bootham Road. Try these:

York Lodge Guest House — Cosy, friendly, ideally located, and well worth £9.50-£10 (about $17). Run by twelve-year-old Christopher and his friendly parents, Hilary and Keith Meadley. At 64 Bootham Crescent, Bootham, York, YO3 7AH, tel. 0904-54289.

The Blossoms — A bigger place, very well-run but less homely, easy to find, and not so expensive, at £8 ($14). (28 Clifton Road, tel. 52391, run by Susan and Chas Bruce.)

Briar Lea Guest House — Small, cosy and friendly. Ray and Judy Sutton, at 8 Longfield Terrace, tel. 0904-35061. £8.50. ($15).

Longfield House — At 2 Longfield Terrace, tel. 0904-27321, run by Mr. & Mrs. Dixon. Good value for £7 ($12).

St. Mary's Hotel — At 17 Longfield Terrace, tel. 76972, run by Mr. & Mrs. Bell, £8.50 ($15) without private bath, £11.50 ($20) with.

Langford House — At 11 St. Mary's, tel. 53573, family-run, car park, TVs in room, wonderful breakfasts, £10 ($17) per person.

Food

For a handy, cheap and historic lunch, try the **King's Manor**, found on Exhibition Square across from the T.I., through the courtyard on the left.(Lunch Mon-Fri 12:00-2:00). Also **Clifton Coin-Op** on Bootham Road between all recommended B&Bs, open Mon-Fri 7:30-8:00, Sat-Sun 7:30-6:00.

TOUR 21
YORK

On this very busy York day we'll start with a good look at its great church, wander through its wonderfully preserved medieval quarter and spend the last half of the day immersed in the past — first reliving the 1800s in the Castle Museum and then going all the way back to the town the Vikings called Jorvik.

Suggested Schedule

9:00 am   Tour York Minster.
10:00 am Browse through old town, Shambles.
1:00 pm   York Castle Museum.
5:00 pm   Jorvik Viking Centre.

Sightseeing highlights

● ● ● **York Minster, or Cathedral** — The pride of York, this largest Gothic church in Britain is thrilling. Pick up the 'Walk Round York Minster' leaflet and ask at the info desk for a guided tour — available almost upon command, and very enlightening. Highlights are the fine medieval stained glass (look at the famous Rose Window in the Chapter House), and the undercroft, showing foundations of Roman and Saxon buildings, the modern concrete save-the-church foundations, the treasure, and a moving display about the recent and tragic 1984 fire and the world-wide support for the restoration work. Open daily from 7:00. Dreary evensong daily at 5:00. Tour info at 24426.

● **The Shambles** — This is the most colourful old York street and the half-timbered core of town. Between there, the Minster and Monk Bar, it's a window-shopper's delight.

● ● ● **York Castle Museum** — Truly one of Europe's top museums, this is a walk with Dickens, the closest thing to a time-tunnel experience you'll ever have. It includes a magnificent collection of old shops well-stocked exactly as they were 150 years ago, costumes, armour, and the 'every home needs one' exhibition, showing the evolution of vacuum cleaners, toilets, TVs, bicycles, cookers, etc from their crude beginnings to now. Cafeteria, shop, car park, open daily 9:30-6:30, Sunday 10:00-6:30, £2 ($3.50), tel. 53611.

● ● **Jorvik** — The new museum of Viking York takes you back 1,000 years — literally backwards — in a little Disney-type train car. Then, still seated, you cruise slowly through the sounds, sights, and even smells of the recreated Viking village of Jorvik with Viking shoes, combs, locks, and other intimate glimpses of their culture. Next you tour the actual excavation site. Located on Coppergate, open daily 9:00-7:00; November-March 9:00-5:30, tel. 643211, £2 ($3.50). To minimise time in the queue — which can be an hour — go early or late.

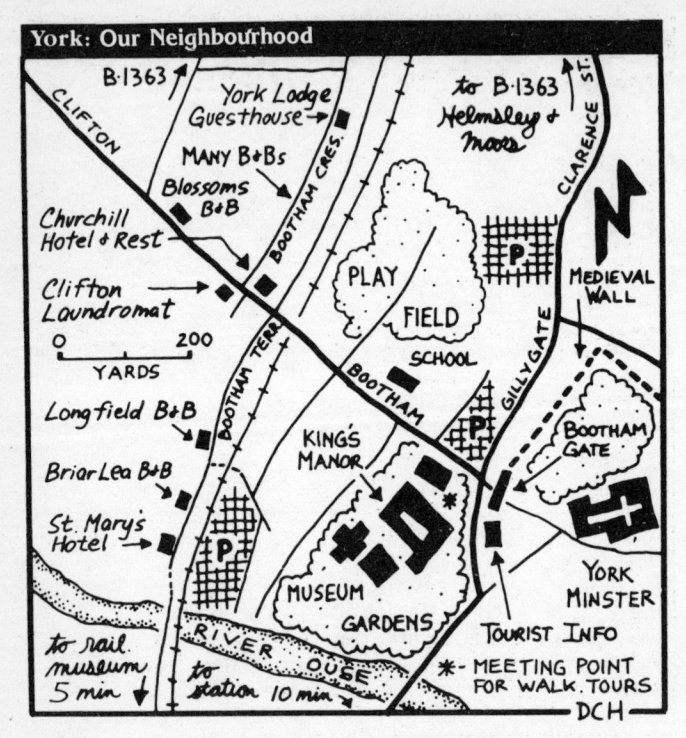

TOUR 22
YORK — CAMBRIDGE — LONDON

On our final day, we'll drive to Cambridge, and probably return our hired car. We'll tour and then savour this historic town, with its famous university and lovely river. After dinner we'll take a quick train journey back to London where we complete our circle of Britain by returning to our hotel of three weeks ago.

Suggested Schedule

9:00 am	Leave York, drive south.
12:00	Arrive Cambridge, leave bags at railway station, return car, book walking tour at T.I., have lunch.
2:15 pm	Walking Tour.
4:15 pm	Free to explore, stroll through Backs, shop in centre, go punting, or take a quick look at the Fitzwilliam Museum paintings.
7:00, 8:14 or 9:50 pm	Take the 70-minute train journey to London (confirm those times at the station). Tube or taxi to your London hotel. Tour over. Everybody off the bus!

Transport

York to Cambridge — Cambridge is a three-hour drive from York. York is such a mess, you'll want to ask at your B&B for the best way to get to the A19 south to Selby. At Selby, cut west on A63 to A1 and follow A1 all the way south to Cambridge. There is a tempting motorway (M1) further west, but stick to the A1 which is near motorway quality and a more interesting drive. (Romantics will be tempted to visit Sherwood Forest, where Robin Hood and his Merry Men took on the rich and powerful so long ago. The Sherwood Forest visitors centre, ten minutes south off the A1 near Edwinstowe north of Nottingham, does its best to resurrect the legend with an exhibition, cafeteria and 'historical' walks in the nearby woods.) Finally, come into Cambridge on the A604, following the signs to the town centre and then to the Tourist Info in Market Place. Driving in Cambridge is another headache. If you need to park, the huge, central Lyon car park is best.

Cambridge to London — From Cambridge, if you're driving to London, any major road going west or south will direct you to the M11 motorway. It's 60 high speed miles (with no petrol stations) to the London ring road. Needless to say, driving in London is no fun. Be sure to catch the poorly marked M25 outer ring road (you'll see Heathrow and Gatwick signs) and circle around to the best position to start your central attack. (You can buy a good London map at the Cambridge T.I., 40p.) If you do decide to drive into London — where your car is a useless headache — you'll learn why I recommend...

Leaving your car in Cambridge — Ideally, you picked up a car at Heathrow that can be dropped at Cambridge. Hertz (Willhire Limited, 41 High Street, Chesterton, tel. 68888), Budget (303 Newmarket Road, 323838), Kenning (47 Coldhams Lane, 61538), Avis (243 Mill Road, 212551), and Godfrey Davis (315 Mill Road, 248198). All the major rental agencies allow you to pick up in Heathrow and drop in Cambridge.

With this plan, you'll drive to the Cambridge railway station to deposit your bags and buy your London ticket, then drop your empty car off at the appropriate agency (see map). From there, take a taxi or one of many Market Square buses to the T.I. to get info and catch the city walk.

After dinner (or during dinner) the train will take you to London's Liverpool Street Station (hourly, 70 minutes journey). Hop on London's handy Central tube line, and return to the hotel you reserved and paid for three weeks earlier.

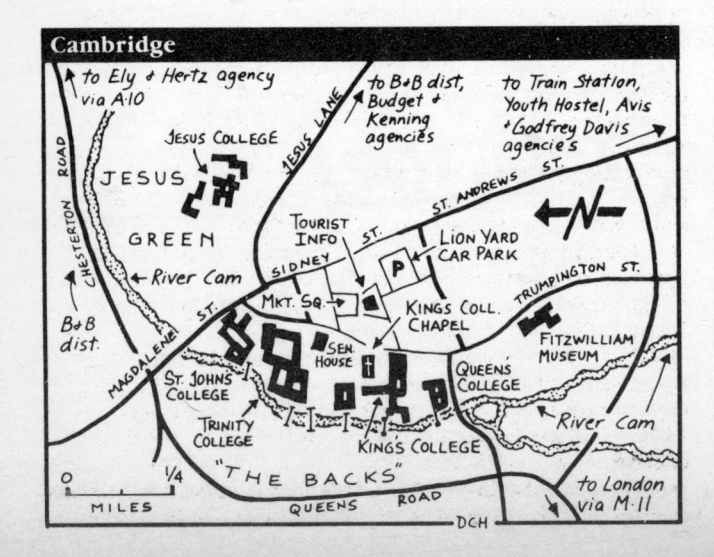

Cambridge
60 miles north of London, this historic town of 100,000 people is world-famous for it prestigious university. Wordsworth, Isaac Newton, Tennyson, Darwin, and Prince Charles are a few products of this busy brainworks. Much more pleasant than its rival, Oxford, Cambridge is the epitome of a university town, with busy bikers, stately halls or residence, plenty of bookshops, and a fun youthfulness permeating its old walls.

Orientation
There's basically one main street separated from the river by the most interesting colleges. The town centre has a handy T.I., colourful marketplace and a much needed huge car park. Everything is a pleasant walk away. Use the Tourist Info (Wheeler Street, tel. 0223-322640, open Monday-Friday, 9:00-6:00; Saturday, 9:00-5:00; Sundays in summer, 10:30-3:30, good room-finding service). Remember, the university dominates — and owns — most of Cambridge. Sightseeing is a bit limited during term time. Approximate term schedule is: January 15-March15, April 15-June 8, October 8-December 8.

Sightseeing highlights
● ● **Walking Tour of the Colleges** — The best way to understand Cambridge's town-gown rivalry and be sure to get a good rundown on the historic and scenic highlights of the university — as well as some fun local gossip — is to take the walking tour. It leaves from the T.I. at 11:00, 1:00, 2:00 and 3:00 in the summer (11:00 and 2:00 off season), £2 ($3.50). Buy tickets or telephone reservations as early that day as you can. If you miss a tour or want your own, private guides are usually on call charging £15 ($26) for the two-hour walk. These tours do their best to work in King's College Chapel and Trinity's Wren Library.

● ● ● **King's College Chapel** — The most impressive single building in town, high Gothic at its best, incredible fan vaulting and Ruben's great Adoration of the Magi. Open 9:30-5:45 daily.

● ● **Trinity College** — The richest and biggest college here, don't miss its great courtyard or the Wren library with its wonderful carving and fascinating manuscripts. Unfortunately, it's only open Monday-Friday 12:00-2:00.

● ● **Fitzwilliam Museum** — The best museum of antiquities and art outside London. Fine Impressionist paintings, old manuscripts, Greek, Egyptian, and Mesopotamian collections. Antiquities open 10:00-2:00, Paintings, 2:00-5:00, everything on Sunday, 2:15-5:00, closed Monday. Free and actually fun.

● **Punting on the Cam** — For a little levity and probably more exercise than you really want, try hiring one of the traditional flat-bottom punts from stalls near either bridge and pole yourself up and down (around and around, more likely) the lazy Cam. Once you get the hang of it, it's a fine way to enjoy the scenic side of Cambridge. After 5:00 it's less crowded.

Accommodation

if you decide to spend the night in Cambridge, you'll be arriving early enough to find a room through the tourist office.

Youth Hostel — The Cambridge hostel is modern, easy-going, friendly, clean, and located near the railway station, a 20-minute walk from the centre. Tel. 354601, at 97 Tenison Road, £5 ($9).

May View Guest House — Perfectly located just off the heavenly Jesus Green and three minutes from the town centre. £8-10 ($14-17) per person, 12 Park Parade, CB5 8AL, tel. 66018.

There are several B&Bs in Jesus Lane (call 60648, 356961, or 353858). Otherwise, most places are farther out in the Chesterton Road area.

Itinerary options

Cambridge is a very easy day trip from London — about an hour each way, round trip rate costing only a little more than one way.

Twenty minutes north of busy Cambridge is the peaceful town of Ely with a stunning cathedral. If you opt for a rest here before the bustle of London, stay at the Black Hostelry, a medieval apartment right in the Cathedral Close courtyard (very quiet). Mr. Green charges £12 ($21) per person. Phone Ely 2612.

Post-tour London

★ Remember to call your airline to reconfirm your return flight three days in advance, leaving your hotel's phone number for any messages.

★ Hopefully you will have thought ahead, taking advantage of the opportunity to reserve hard-to-get tickets at the start of the trip to enjoy a special show or event before returning home.

★ Ask at your hotel for the easiest way to the airport. To Gatwick, take the shuttle train from Victoria Station. To Heathrow, take the tube or the Airbus. Airbus is easiest, dropping you right at terminal 3 for international departures (£3 ($5)). Taxis are a ripoff from airports, but two or three people in a hurry can travel reasonably from the West End out. I flagged down a cab while waiting for the Airbus and negotiated a £10 ($17) ride from Holland Park to Heathrow.

★ Phone before going to the airport to check for delays.

★ Phone home (50p or a pound is enough) to say all's well and what time you're due in.

POST-TOUR OPTION: IRELAND

The obvious gap in this itinerary is Ireland. I agonised over what to do with the friendly Emerald Isle. I love Ireland. Most who visit do. But it doesn't make it into the top 22 days. Still, Ireland is easy to work in as a side trip or finale to this plan. Here are a few points to consider.

Itinerary strategy — getting there
Ireland can be inserted into the itinerary from North Wales. Boats sail from Holyhead to Dun Laoghaire three or four times a day (3½ hour trip, £20 ($35), get a ticket ASAP in London). Ask about cheap round trip tickets. The train/boat London-Dublin journey costs about £35 ($60), overnight or all day. Coaches go daily between Glasgow and Belfast (10-12 hours £15 ($25)).

Consider an open-ended flight plan, flying into London and home from Shannon Airport in Western Ireland. Your itinerary then would be: London, Wales, England, Scotland, Belfast, Dublin, West Ireland, fly home.

If you'll be touring the Continent with a Eurail pass, start it in Ireland (it's good on Irish trains and many buses) and travel free on the otherwise expensive 24-hour boat trip to France. (Note: This trip can be rough. Upon boarding, those concerned about seasickness should go straight to the ship's cafeteria and eat a small plastic tub full of strawberry jelly. While this won't stop the nausea, it helps the aftertaste.)

Transport in Ireland
For a quick visit to Dublin and a day tour into the countryside you'll just take the boat and catch a bus tour in Dublin. For a more extensive visit, here are your options. Irish trains are expensive and not extensive, with meagre schedules and coverage. British Rail passes don't work here. The bus is cheaper with better coverage. Study special passes; students get a 50% discount with ISIC cards. Taking a car from England is complicated and expensive. Most people rent a separate car (by the week) from home for Ireland. Hitchhiking is the best in Europe, very safe. You'll make more friends, spend less money.

Sightseeing highlights
Dublin — Not a favourite city of mine but worth a day. Compact centre around O'Connell Street Bridge and the River Liffy. Boats land at nearby Dun Laoghaire with good bus connections into Dublin. Tourist Info at 14 Upper O'Connell Street, tel. 747733, open Monday-Saturday 8:30-6:00, has good room-finding services. Orientate yourself with a city walking tour.

Visit Trinity College (stately grounds, historic buildings, illuminated Book of Kells manuscript); the National Museum (moving exhibition of the 1916 Rebellion, impressive medieval and earlier Irish artifacts, open Tue-Sat 10:00-5:00, Sunday 2:00-5:00); General Post Office (unimpressive building but it's the site of the 1916 proclamation of the Independent Irish Republic); Kilmainham Jail (symbol of the Irish struggle against Britain, martyr memorabilia, open Wednesday 10:00-12:00, 2:30-4:00, and Sunday 3:00-5:00 only); Guinness Brewery (video show, free beer, Mon-Fri 10:00-3:00).

For entertainment, sample the great Irish theatre (Abbey Theatre and many others, shows Mon-Sat 8:00 pm), seek out some Irish folk music in a local pub, or discover some Irish sports — hurling (the rugged national sport that's like airborne hockey), or Gaelic football (a violent form of rugby). Games

Post Tour Option: Ireland

nearly every Sunday at Dublin's Croke Park. Use the periodical entertainment guide 'In Dublin' for music, theatre, sports and tour listings.

Glendalough — The best short day trip from Dublin for a sample of rural Ireland is into the Wicklow mountains to Glendalough. 1,500 years ago the hermit St. Kevin established a thriving monastic school here. Today its ruins surrounded by scenic forests and lakes are understandably popular with tourists. Look into a one-day tour with a local company.

Belfast — Just a direct three-hour train ride north, this embattled capital of the North offers a safe and fascinating look at 'The Troubles'. You'll be frisked at the checkpoint and then step into the traffic-free 'safe-zone'. Browse through a bomb damage clearance sale. Take a side trip south to the wonderful Cultra Open Air Folk Museum, talk to the people. With common sense (don't sing Catholic songs in Protestant pubs), Belfast is as safe as London. See the chapter on Belfast in *Europe Through the Back Door*. Consider a Belfast-Glasgow coach connection.

Wexford-Rosslare Harbour — Visit this area only to catch the boat to South Wales or France.

Cork — Ireland's rough, but pleasant, second city. Boat to France (free on Eurail pass) and near the famous Blarney Castle with its too-famous Blarney Stone (that hordes of tourists kiss to get the 'gift of gab').

Cashel — A stirring religious and political centre from the mysterious days of St. Patrick. Fine Celtic cross graveyard, good tours, open daily 9:00-7:30, 10:30-4:30 in winter. Two buses a day to and from Dublin and Cork.

Dingle Peninsula — My favourite scenery in the British isles is Ireland's West Coast. And the best in the West is the rugged beauty of hearty Dingle Peninsula — just north of the very touristy Ring of Kerry. Dingle is a Gaeltacht — a region where the locals still speak the old Irish or Gaelic language. This is a cultural preserve with traditional dress, music, and lifestyles complementing the natural beauty. (See *Europe Through the Back Door* chapter on Dingle.) Train to the pleasant town of Tralee, then bus or thumb to Dingle town. Set up at Mrs. Farrell's Corner House (tel. 066 51516). Rent a bike for the circular trip out to Slea Head (incredible scenery, villages, explore the medieval monks' stone beehive huts, or clochans, along the way) but be home in time to catch the nightly folk music at O'Flaherty's Pub.

Galway — Largest city in the west. Cosy, historic, 3½ hours by train to and from Dublin and Cork, direct bus to Rosslare. Daily boats and cheap flights to the Aran Islands (try for any kind of discount you can dream up).

Aran Islands — Off the coast of Galway, this tiny group of wave-whipped islands is a stark and traditional outpost of Irish culture and is not terribly touristy. Spend two days on the main island, rent bikes and explore. Boats connect islands with the mainland. One goes to Doolin, home of Ireland's best folk music — but not much else.

Donegal — Ireland in the extreme, the cultural caricature of this lush island where everyone seems to be typecast for an Irish film. Enter Donegal with caution, for while it has no real 'sights' it is seductive and many unwary visitors end up skipping the rest of their itinerary. One American accountant 'called in well' and was never seen again.

Suggested Itinerary

Quick Ireland, spliced in from North Wales:

Day 1	Leave hired car at Holyhead, take boat to Dun Laoghaire, set up in Dublin.
Day 2	Sightsee Dublin.
Day 3	Sidetrip south to Glendalough and Wicklow Mountains.
Day 4	Early boat back to Holyhead, pick up car or train, and go to Blackpool.

Longer Ireland:

Revise your main itinerary as if returning to London on the overnight train from Scotland (London-Bath-North Wales-York-Edinburgh). Return car in Edinburgh if driving.

Day 21	Edinburgh — Glasgow — Coach/Boat — Belfast.
Day 22	Sightsee in Belfast, afternoon at Cultra Folk Museum.
Day 23	Early train to Dublin, sightsee all day there.
Day 24	Dublin — Cashel — Tralee — Dingle.
Day 25	Dingle, bike the peninsula.
Day 26	Dingle — Tralee — Shannon Airport to fly home; or Dingle — Dublin, and night train/boat back to London.

Post Tour Option: Ireland

Helpful hints

Understand Ireland's 'Troubles' — the North-South, Catholic-Protestant problem. A fine background and wonderful reading is *Trinity* by Leon Uris.

Ireland is very small (about 150 by 200 miles) but it has no English-style motorways. Travelling is slow. Approach every trip as a joyride. Travelling in Ireland is generally cheaper than in England. Ireland's pound is worth much less than the British pound.

The Irish B&Bs are even cosier and less expensive than England's and travelling without reservations is not difficult. Use the *Let's Go: Britain and Ireland* guide book.

You'll find that Ireland's weather ranges from damp to drizzly to downpour and her people are her main attraction. You can't enjoy Ireland without enjoying her people.

PRACTICAL EXTRAS

Sleeping in Britain

Thank God Britain has such lousy hotels. Because the alternative — bed and breakfast places — is second-to-none, with a homely charm that I'd prefer to even the most luxurious European hotels. Generally, the less atmosphere a hotel has, the more it charges. But guesthouses and bed and breakfasts seem to be popping up all over the place to fill that void.

On this trip I'm assuming you have a reasonable but limited budget. Skip hotels. Go the B&B (bed and breakfast) way. Where there's a demand, there will be a supply. B&Bs put up their signs where you need them, and any town with tourists has a tourist office that can book one for you or give you a list and point you in the right direction. Without a T.I. (Tourist Information office), ask people on the street for help.

B&Bs are family run, usually just a large home with a few extra rooms to let. They charge from £7-£10 ($12-17) and always include the 'full English breakfast'. How much cosiness and extra tea and biscuits is tossed in varies tremendously.

The B&Bs I've recommended are nearly all stocking-feet comfortable and very homely. My prerequisites for recommending a place are: friendly; in a central, safe, quiet neighbourhood; clean, with good beds, a basin in room and shower down the hall; not in other guidebooks and therefore filled mostly by English travellers, and willing to hold a room until 4:00-6:00 pm without a deposit. (In certain cases my recommendations don't meet all these prerequisites.)

I promised the owners of the places I list that you would be reliable when you made a telephone reservation — please don't let these people (or me) down. If you'll be delayed or won't make it, phone. They can normally fill your bed only with the help of the local tourist office room-finding service which usually closes at 5:00 or 6:00. Tourists are notorious for 'standing up' B&Bs.

A few tips: B&B proprietors are selective in who they invite in for the night. Risky-looking people find many places suddenly full. If you'll be staying for more than one night you are a 'desirable'. Sometimes staying several nights earns you a better price — ask about it. The T.I. generally takes about a 10% commission for those they send. If you book direct, the B&B gets it all. Nearly all B&Bs have plenty of stairs. Expect good exercise and be happy you packed light. If one B&B is full, ask for guidance. (Mention this book..) Owners usually work together and can call up an ally to land you a bed. Unless I'm relying on a particular recommendation, I enjoy shopping for my B&B, touring three places and choosing the best. 'Twin' and 'double' are two entirely different things. If you'll take two single beds or a double bed say so or you may be needlessly turned away. B&Bs advertise with prominent signs in the garden or windows.

Room-finding is very easy from mid-September to early June. Otherwise phone ahead, try to arrive early and take advantage of room-finding services in most tourist offices. They charge about a pound for reservations in another city but can save you lots of headaches.

Youth Hostels: Britain has four hundred youth hostels — of all shapes and sizes. They can be historic castles or depressing huts, serene and comfy or overrun by noisy children, but they're never expensive.

Hostels charge about £4 ($6) a night and normally provide hot meals at budget prices and a member's kitchen for even cheaper eating. They are generally wonderfully located and pleasantly run, but hostels are not B&Bs. You need a membership card, there's a dormitory for men and one for women. They lock up through mid-day and usually at 11:00 pm. Big city hostels are normally more chaotic and less comfortable than town and country ones. Off-season hostelling is easy and so uncrowded that married couples can often share a room. In peak season, most hostels fill up by dinnertime. There is absolutely no age limit to hostelling. In fact, there's a new membership card giving youth hostellers over the age of sixty a discount. Many English hostellers have been at it for 50 years. Use the British hostel guidebook, available at any hostel. If you're travelling alone, this is the best way to defeat hotel loneliness. Hostels are also a tremendous source of local and budget travel information. If you hostel selectively you'll enjoy historical and very interesting buildings.

Eating in Britain

I think English food is just fine. But then, I liked school meals too. True, England isn't famous for its cuisine and it probably never will be, but we tourists have to eat. And, if there's any good place to cut corners to stretch your budget in Britain, it's in eating. Here are a few tips on budget eating in Britain.

The English (or Scottish or Welsh) 'fry' is famous as a hearty way to start the day. Also know as a 'plate of cardiac arrest', the breakfast is especially feasty if you've just come from the lands of the skimpy continental breakfast across the Channel.

The standard B&B breakfast starts with fruit juice and cereal (or porridge). Top-notch places give both and occasionally even grapefruit sections. There are usually several cereals. Scotland serves great porridge. Then, with tea or coffee, you get a heated plate with a fried egg, very lean bacon, a pretty bad sausage, a grilled tomato, and often a slice of delightfully greasy fried bread and sauteed mushrooms. The last course is a rack of toast with butter and marmalade. This meal tides many travellers over until dinner.

One problem with B&Bs and this itinerary is than many don't serve until 8:30 or 9:00. If you need an early start, ask politely if it's possible. Consider skipping breakfast on occasion if a quick start is important.

For lunch on this tour I'd picnic. Restaurants cost too much time and money. Pack your car with a backseat cardboard pantry. Our standard shopping list includes: boxes of orange juice (Del Monte is best), fresh bread, tasty English cheese, meat, a tube of Coleman's English mustard, local eating apples, bananas, small tomatoes, chocolate-covered 'Digestive' sweet biscuits, savoury biscuits or crackers, nuts, paper towels, and any local specialities we bump into. English open-air markets and supermarkets are fine. We often eat 'meals on wheels' en route to save 30 precious minutes and enjoy a relaxed-paced meal as we drive. A small plastic water bottle, sandwich bags and a Swiss army knife are handy.

Pub grub — Pubs offer the best basic budget dinner in friendly surroundings. Pubs generally serve assorted meat pies (steak and kidney pie, shepherd's pie, etc) curried dishes, fish, quiche and vegetables — invariably chips and peas. Servings are hearty, service is quick and dinners cost from £1.50-£3.00 ($2.50-$6.00). Your pint of beer or cider adds another 60p or so. Free water is always available. A 'ploughman's lunch' is a modern 'traditional' English meal that nearly every tourist tries...once.

Beer — The British take great pride in their beer. They think that drinking beer cold and carbonated as foreigners do ruins the taste. If you are not used to it, a good English beer tastes flat, smooth and room temperature. Experiment with the English 'bitters', ales and local brews. Stick to whatever's on tap and try the draught cider cautiously. And if you can't acquire a taste for the local brew, ask for a lager.

Pub hours vary, but they are usually open 11:00-3:00 and 6:30-11:00 pm. Drinks are served by the pint or the half-pint (not macho for a man to order just a half). Teetotallers can order soft drinks or a 'shandy'. 'Pub' is short for 'public house' — go there to be social. They're the next best thing to relatives in every town.

Other budget meals — While English restaurants are fairly expensive, there are plenty of cheap alternatives: fish 'n' chips joints, Chinese take-aways, cafeterias, B&Bs that serve evening meals, and your typical good old 'greasy spoon' places.
Throughout Britain I've had very good luck following the recommendations of my B&Bs.

Money

Foreign visitors used to find British currency confusing in pre-decimal days — it insisted on units which were impossible to calculate. Nowadays it is much simpler. Coins range from 1p to £1 and notes from £5 to £50.

Scotland and Ireland have their own currencies. English and Scottish money are worth the same and are good in both countries (but it can be troublesome to spend Scottish currency in England). The Irish-English money relationship is more complex. English money is a little more valuable. Treat Ireland as a different country (which it is).

Britain has a 15% sales tax that is called a 'value added tax', or 'VAT'. This is built into nearly everything you buy. Tourists can get a refund on this VAT on souvenirs they take out of the country but it's a major headache. Unless you buy something worth several hundred pounds, your refund won't be worth the delays, incidental expenses, and headaches that complicate the lives of TISVATR (Tourists In Search of VAT Refunds).

Even in jolly old England, you should use travellers cheques and a money belt. Theft is a part of tourism and the meek may be blessed but the careless are sitting ducks. A moneybelt is peace of mind.

If you'll be travelling exclusively in Great Britain, buy travellers cheques in pounds sterling. If you get Barclays cheques you'll find a Barclays Bank in nearly every English town, sometimes avoiding the commission banks charge for changing money. I bring a credit card only because it's necessary to hire a car. Spend cash — not plastic — as you travel. Save time and money by changing plenty of money at a time. With a money belt you can carry several hundred pounds (worth of money) safely.

Britain may be decimalised, but it is not yet fully metricated. The British use Fahrenheit, miles, inches, pounds and ounces.

Driving British

Driving in Britain is basically wonderful — if you remember that the rules of the road may not be the same as you are used to. It's really very easy if you want it to be. Here are a few random tips.

An AA membership (Automobile Association) comes with most hired cars. Be sure you know how it works. Petrol is about £1.70 ($3) per gallon and self-serve. Know what octane rating your car takes, push the correct button and pump away. (Over 3,000 miles on my last trip I paid 5 pence per mile for petrol.) Seatbelts are required by law in the front seats.

Speed limits are 30 mph in town, 70 on the motorways and 60 elsewhere. Time estimates in this book assume a law-abiding speed. Avoid big cities whenever possible. Most have modern ring roads to skirt the congestion. Rush hours are basically the same in most countries. The shortest distance between any two points is almost always the motorway.

Parking is confusing. One yellow line means no parking Monday—Saturday during working hours. Double yellow lines mean no parking ever. Broken yellow means short stops are okay, but always look for explicit signs or ask a passer-by.

Copy your car key as soon as possible so you won't get locked out and so your partner enjoys access to the car. Buy something to clean your windows with each morning. If want other drivers to give you a wide berth, pick up a red 'L' sign at a motorists' shop. Display it on the back of your car and you'll be feared like any 'Learner' should be.

Great Britain by train and coach

Britain has a great train and coach system, and travellers who don't want to (or can't afford to) drive a hire car can enjoy an exciting holiday using public transport. But you'll lose a lot of control, and Britain, more than any other European country, lends itself to car travel.

A train/coach trip requires some tailoring to avoid areas that are difficult without your own wheels and to take advantage of certain bonuses train travel offers. Consider a plan like this:

Britain by Train	
Day 1	Arrive in London
Day 2	London
Day 3	London
Day 4	Bath
Day 5	Side trip to Wells and Glastonbury
Day 6	Cardiff, St Fagans, to Cheltenham
Day 7	Explore Cotswolds with Cheltenham as a base
Day 8	Stratford, Warwick
Day 9	Coventry to North Wales
Day 10	North Wales
Day 11	North Wales — Blackpool
Day 12	Blackpool — York
Day 13	York
Day 14	York — Durham — Hadrian's Wall — Edinburgh
Day 15	Edinburgh
Day 16	Edinburgh
Day 17	Edinburgh — Mallaig
Day 18	Isle of Skye — Inverness, night train to London
Day 19	London — side trip to Cambridge
Day 20	Side trip from London to Salisbury, Stonehenge
Day 21	Free day
Day 22	Free day to insert where needed.

London is the hub, with speedy commuter trains going everywhere. Remember, London has many stations, each serving a general region. Round-trip 'day return' tickets are just a bit more than one-way fares, making day-trips to places like Cambridge, Salisbury, Stonehenge, Oxford, Stratford and Bath reasonable. **London to Salisbury** (80 miles from Waterloo Station, 90 minutes, hourly), **Salisbury to Stonehenge** (9 miles, 30 minutes bus ride changing at Amesbury, several a day from town centre or station), **London to Bath** (from Paddington Station, 90 minutes, hourly). Note: All times and schedules listed in this chapter work the same in both directions.

Bath — Most longer journeys change at Bristol (15 minutes from Bath, four times an hour).

Bristol to Cardiff (60 minutes, hourly). Bath railway info — 63075, coach info — 64446.

Cardiff — The transport hub of South Wales. Buses direct to St Fagan's and Caerphilly. Train to Cheltenham (80 minutes, every two hours). Railway info — 28000, bus info — 371331.

Cheltenham — The Cotswolds are hiking, biking or driving country but a few train lines and sporadic bus service will get you around if necessary. Cheltenham, from a public transport point of view, is your best base. Be sure to pick up the 'Cotswold Bus and Rail Guide' there. **Cheltenham — Birmingham** (hourly, 45 minutes). Train info — 29501, bus info — 22021, Cheltenham tourist info — 522878.

Stratford — Warwick — Coventry. This segment of the trip is so easy by car but messy otherwise. Birmingham is the transport hub of this region and each place is well served from Birmingham. **Stratford to Warwick** (train and bus almost hourly, 20 minutes), **to Coventry** (bus almost hourly, 75 minutes), **to London** (8 trains a day, 2¼ hours). Train info — 204444, bus info — 204181. Tour companies make day tripping from Stratford to Blenheim, Oxford, Cotswolds, Warwick and Coventry possible — but not cheap. **Coventry** — Bus 25 connects the bus and train stations going through the centre of town past the cathedral and tourist info. National Express (tel. 730-0202) offers 12-hour day trips from London to Coventry and Warwick for £10 ($17).

Iron Bridge Gorge — This birthplace of the Industrial Revolution is still in the Stone Age, transport wise. It's too difficult without a car and, for most, not worth the trouble.

North Wales — The plan in this book won't work without a car but North Wales has good and scenic trains and buses. You can pick up plenty of info locally and a special 'Day Rover' ticket gives you a day of buses quite cheaply. **Chester — Holyhead** train (6-8 times a day, two hours). **Caernarfon — Blaenau Ffestiniog** (bus every two hours). Look into the old miniature-gauge Ffestiniog railway.

Chester — Crewe — Preston — Blackpool. This is England's industrial heartland, and trains are very frequent. With the two changes, this journey should take three hours.

Blackpool — Manchester (two per hour, 90 minutes).

Manchester — York (leaving at 28 past each hour, 90 minutes).

Lake District is frustrating for those with limited time and no car. There are buses and trains serving the area, but I'd skip it.

York and **Edinburgh** are very well connected by train (hourly

trips, three hours). That train stops in Durham and Newcastle.
York-London (hourly, two hours long). Train info 25671, coach
info 24161.

Durham — Newcastle (four trains per hour, 15 minutes). Tour
Hadrian's Wall from Newcastle. The Newcastle — Carlisle train is
very scenic, stopping at Hexham and Haltwhistle and going right
along the Wall (hourly, 90 minutes). In the summer there's a
tourist-oriented coach service four times a day from Newcastle.

Edinburgh — To get to the rugged west and islands from
Edinburgh you go via **Glasgow** (trains from Edinburgh twice an
hour, 50 minutes) or **Inverness** (four times a day, 3½ hours).
Edinburgh has plenty of reasonably priced organised coach tours
covering Loch Ness, Oban, Isle of Mull and Inverness.

Glasgow — Oban train (3 hours, three a day), **Glasgow — Mallaig** (6 hours with an hour break in Fort William, three a
day), **Kyle of Lochalsh — Inverness** (2½ hours, three a day).
Edinburgh train info — 556-2451, coach info — 556-8464.

Overnight train back to London: **Inverness — London**
(19:30 — 6:47, 20:30 — 7:32 each night), a sleeping berth is a
good investment. Inverness train info — 232651, coach info —
233371.

A trip of this...ferocity...justifies a BritRail Pass. These passes
give you unlimited rail travel in England, Scotland and Wales.
You must buy it outside Great Britain (ideally, from your travel
agent). The promotional info is a bit complicated, but very
thorough. Read it carefully. For more info, including British Rail
network map, write to your nearest Britrail Travel International
Office.

British coaches are cheaper but slower than trains. They will
take you where the trains don't. Stations are often at or near
train stations. Be aware of the distinction between 'buses' (for
local runs with lots of stops) and 'coaches' (long distance,
express runs). If your budget is very tight, you can save plenty
by skipping the BritRail Pass in favour of the Brit-Express Pass
which gives you unlimited travel on the National Express coaches
(15 days for about £45 ($80), 22 days for about £60 ($100),
through your travel agent or in London — tel. 730-0202).

Of course you could do this whole trip hitchhiking. It would
take more time but you'd make a lot more friends. If you plan to
use your thumb get a hitching guidebook (try *Hitch Hikers
Manual: Britain*, £3.95 ($7), from Vacation Work, 9 Park End St.
Oxford OX1 1HJ, or *A Hitch-Hiker's Guide to Great Britain*,
Penguin, £2.95 ($5)).

Getting to London — fly!

Flying to London is your major expense, and a little study can
save you a fortune. Fares and regulations to England vary from

country to country, and even within countries. Wherever you are, it is a good idea to shop around, and find a good travel agent. You need an agent who knows and enjoys budget European travel. Read the newspapers, talk to other travellers, but most of all establish a loyal relationship with a good agent. London is usually the cheapest European destination from many countries, and if you can avoid summer travel it's even cheaper.

The 'Open to View' ticket

Many foreign tourists jump on special coupons, all-you-can-eat meals and clever gimmicks that sound so good. After your plane ticket, BritRail Pass, and car hire (which can be cheaper from home) nearly anything you buy at home is a bad deal that will do more complicating that simplifying.

This is also true for the 'Open to View' ticket, which gives you free entry for a month to hundreds of Britain's top sights. It costs only £16 in the UK so don't buy it until you get to London. The Heathrow and Victoria station tourist offices issue them on the spot.

On this itinerary, the OTV covers: Tower of London (£3), Stonehenge (£1), Tintern Abbey (90p), Blenheim Palace (£2), Warwick Castle (£3.25), Caernafon Castle (£1.60), Urquhart Castle (£1), Culloden (£1), Edinburgh Castle (£2), Georgian House (£1), Gladstones Land (£1), Housesteads Roman Fort (£1), Roman Baths in Bath (£1), Holyrood Palace (£1), and several other sights you may see. Total value — £22, your cost £16 — and you only feel the pain once. Get it.

Festivals

Jousting Tournament of Knights, last Sun & Mon in May at Chilham Castle near Canterbury, Medieval pageantry, colourful.
Allington Castle Medieval Market, 2nd or 3rd Sat in June in Maidstone (30 mi. SE. of London). Medieval crafts and entertainment.
Druid Summer Soltice Ceremonies, June 20 or 21, Stonehenge. Hoods and white robes, rituals from midnight to sunrise at about 4:45 am.
Alnwick Medieval Fair, last Sun in June to next Sat. Medieval costumes, competition, entertainment. Alnwick, 30 mi. N. of Newcastle.
Haslemere Early Music Festival, 2 Fridays before 4th Sat in July. 16th-18th century music on original instruments. 40 mi. S. of London.
Sidmouth International Folklore Festival, 1st to 2nd Fridays in August, 300 events, 15 mi. E. of Exeter.
Reading Rock Festival, last weekend of August. England's best. 40 mi. W. of London.

Nottingham Goose Fair, 1st Thurs-Sat in Oct, one of England's oldest and largest fairs. Nottingham.

CULTURAL INSIGHTS FOR TRAVELLERS

What's so Great about Britain?

For its size, Britain probably has more world-famous tourist attractions than any other country.

Britain is small — about the size of Uganda — 600 miles long and 300 at its widest. Its highest mountain is 4,400 feet — a foothill by most standards — the population is a quarter of the USA's and, politically and economically, the Great Britain closing out the 20th century is a shadow of the days when it boasted 'The sun never sets on the British Empire'.

At one time Britain owned one-fifth of the world and accounted for over half the planet's industrial output. Today the Empire is down to titbits like the Falklands and Gibraltar, and her industrial production is but a small proportion of the world's total.

Still, Britain is a world leader. Her heritage, her culture and her people cannot be measured in traditional units of power.

The United Kingdom of Great Britain and Northern Ireland is a union of four countries — England, Wales, Scotland and Northern Ireland. Cynics call it an English Empire ruled by London, and there is some tension between the dominant Anglo-Saxon English (46 million) and their Celtic brothers (10 million).

In the Dark Ages, the Angles moved into this region from Europe pushing the Celtic inhabitants to the undesirable fringe of the islands. The Angles settled in Angle-land (England) while the Celts made do in Wales, Scotland and Ireland.

Today Wales, with 2½ million people, struggles along with a terrible economy, dragged down by the depressed mining industry. There is a great deal of Welsh pride apparent in the local music and in the bilingual signs. 500,000 people speak the Welsh language.

Scotland is big, taking up one-third of Britain, but is sparsely inhabited by only 5½ million people. Only about 80,000 speak Gaelic (the old Scottish language) but the Scots enjoy a large measure of autonomy with their separate Church of Scotland, their own legal system and Scottish currency. Scotland is allowed to pretty much run its own domestic affairs. Its economy is sagging, but the recent North Sea oil boom has been a great shot in the Scottish arm.

Ireland, the island west of England, is divided. Most of it is the completely independent and Catholic Republic of Ireland. The top quarter is Northern Ireland — ruled from London. Long ago the Protestant English and Scots moved into the north, the industrial heartland of Ireland, and told the Catholic Irish to 'go to Hell or go to Connemara'. They moved to the bleak and less productive parts of the island, and the seeds of today's 'Troubles' were planted. There's no easy answer or easy blame, but that island has struggled — its population is only a third (3 million) of what it used to be — and the battle continues.

As a visitor today, you'll see a politically polarised England. The Conservatives, with Margaret Thatcher at the helm, are taking a right-wing approach to Britain's serious problems, returning to Victorian values — community, family, hard work and thrift. The Labour and Liberal parties see an almost irreparable break-up of the social service programmes so dear to them.

British history for the traveller

When Julius Caeser landed on the misty and mysterious isle of Britain in 55 BC, England entered the history books. The primitive Celtic tribes he conquered were themselves invaders who had earlier conquered the even more mysterious people who built Stonehenge in prehistoric times.

The Romans built towns and roads (including Watling Street and Fosse Way which remain today) and established their capital at 'Londinium'. The Celtic natives, consisting of 'Gaels', 'Picts' and 'Scots', were not subdued so easily in what is present-day Scotland and Wales, and the Romans had to build Hadrian's Wall near the Scottish border to keep invading Scots out. Even today, the Celtic language and influence are strongest in the Gael-ic and Scot-tish regions.

As Rome fell, so fell Roman Britain — a victim of invaders and internal troubles. Barbarian tribes from Germany and Denmark called Angles and Saxons swept through the southern part of the island, establishing 'Angle-land'. These were the days of the real King Arthur, probably a Christianised Roman general fighting valiantly but vainly against invading barbarians. The island was plunged into 500 years of Dark Ages — wars, plagues and poverty — lit only by the dim candle of a few learned Christian monks and missionaries trying to convert the barbarians.

Modern England began with yet another invasion. William the Conqueror and his Norman troops crossed the Channel from France in 1066. He crowned himself king in Westminster Abbey (as all subsequent royalty would) and began building the Tower of London. French-speaking Norman kings ruled the country for two centuries.

With their fall, the country suffered through two more centuries of civil wars, with various noble families vying for the crown. In one of the most bitter feuds, the York and Lancaster families fought the 'Wars of the Roses', so-called because of the white and red flowers they chose as their symbols. Battles; intrigues; kings, nobles and ladies imprisoned and executed in the Tower — it's a wonder the country survived its rulers.

The country was finally united by the 'third-party' Tudor family.

Henry VIII, a Tudor, was England's Renaissance king. He was handsome, athletic, a poet, a scholar and a musician. He was also arrogant, cruel, gluttonous and paranoid. He went through six wives in forty years, divorcing, imprisoning or beheading them when they no longer suited his needs. Henry also 'divorced' England from the Catholic Church, establishing the Protestant Church of England (Anglican Church) and setting in motion years of years of religious squabbles. Henry also 'dissolved' the monasteries, leaving just the shells of many formerly glorious abbeys dotting the countryside.

Henry's daughter, Queen Elizabeth I, made England a great naval and trading power and presided over the 'Elizabethan era' of great writers, including Shakespeare.

The long-standing quarrel between England's kings and nobles in Parliament finally erupted into a Civil War (1650). Parliament forces under the Puritan farmer Oliver Cromwell defeated — and beheaded — King Charles I. This Civil War left its mark on much of what you'll see in England. Eventually, Parliament invited Charles' son to retake the throne. This Restoration of the monarchy was accompanied by a great rebuilding of London (including Christopher Wren's St. Paul's Cathedral), which had been devastated by the Great Fire of 1666.

Britain grew as a great naval power, colonising and trading with all parts of the globe. Her naval superiority ('Britannia rules the waves') was secured by Admiral Nelson's victory over Napoleon's fleet at the Battle of Trafalgar while Lord Wellington squashed Napoleon on land at Waterloo. Nelson and Wellington are memoralised by many arches, columns, squares, etc throughout England.

Economically, Britain led the world into the Industrial Age with her mills, factories, coal mines and trains. By the time of Queen Victoria's reign (1837-1901), Britain was at the zenith of power with a colonial empire that covered one-fifth of the world.

The Twentieth Century has not been kind to Britain, however. Two World Wars devastated the population. The Nazi 'Blitz' reduced much of London to rubble. Her colonial empire has dwindled to almost nothing and the economy is plagued by strikes, inflation and unemployment. The 'Irish Troubles' are a constant thorn as the Catholic inhabitants of British-ruled Northern Ireland fight for the same independence their southern neighbours won decades ago. The recent war over the Falkland Islands showed how little of the British Empire there is left, but also how determined the British are to hang on to what remains.

The tradition of greatness continues unbowed, however, presided over by Queen Elizabeth II, her husband Prince Philip (the Duke of Edinburgh), the heir-apparent the Prince of Wales (Prince Charles), whose wife is still popularly known as Lady Di.

Cultural Insights for Travellers

The pomp and circumstance surrounding the recent wedding of Prince Andrew and Sarah Ferguson (now the Duke and Duchess of York) shows how much the trappings of the monarchy mean to the British people.

Architecture in Britain

From Stonehenge to Big Ben, travellers are going to be storming castle walls, climbing spiral staircases and snapping the pictures of 5,000 years of architecture. Let's sort it out.

The oldest stuff — mysterious and prehistoric — goes from before Roman times back to 3,000 BC. The earliest — like Stonehenge and Avebury — is from the Stone and Bronze Ages. The remains from this period are made of huge stones or mounds of earth, even manmade hills, and were built for worship or burial. Iron Age people (600 BC to 400 AD) left us desolate hill forts.

The Romans thrived in Britain from 50 to 400 AD, building cities, walls, and roads. Evidence of Roman greatness can be seen in lavish villas with ornate mosaic floors, temples uncovered beneath great English churches and Roman stones in medieval city walls. Roman roads sliced across the island in straight lines. Today any unusually straight small rural road is very likely laid directly on an ancient Roman road.

Roman Britain crumbled in the fifth century and there was little building in Dark Age England. Architecturally, the light was switched on with the Norman Conquest in 1066. As William earned his title 'the Conqueror', he built churches and castles in the European Romanesque style.

English Romanesque is called 'Norman'. The round arches and strong, simple and stocky Norman style (1050-1200) made churches that were fortress-like with thick walls, small windows and crenellations. Durham Cathedral and the Chapel of St. John in the Tower of London are typical Norman churches. The Tower of London with its square keep, small windows and spiral stone stairways is a typical Norman castle. You'll see plenty of Norman castles — all built to secure the conquest of these invaders from Normandy.

Gothic architecture (1200-1600) replaced the heavy Norman style with light and vertical buildings, pointed arches, tall soaring spires and bigger windows. English Gothic is divided into three stages. Early English (1200-1300) features tall simple spires, beautifully carved capitals, and elaborate chapter houses (eg Salisbury and Wells cathedrals). Decorated Gothic (1300-1370) gets fancier with more elaborate tracery, bigger windows, and ornately carved pinnacles, as you'll see at Westminster Abbey. Finally, the Perpendicular style (1370-1600) goes back to square towers and emphasises straight uninterrupted verticle lines from ceiling to floor with vast windows and exuberant decoration including fan vaulted ceilings (King's College Chapel at Cambridge).

As you tour the great medieval churches of England, remember, nearly everything is symbolic. Local guides give regular tours, and books also help us modern pilgrims understand at least a little of what we see. For instance, on the tombs, if the figure has crossed legs, he was a crusader. If his feet rest on a dog he died at home, but if the legs rest on a lion he died in battle.

There aren't many Gothic castles. The rulers seem to have needed castles only to subdue the stubborn Welsh. Edward I built a ring of powerful castles in Wales (like Caernarfon and Conway) to deal with the Welsh.

Gothic houses were a simple mix of woven strips of thin wood, rubble and plaster called wattle and daub. The famous black and white Tudor, or half-timbered look, was simply heavy oak frames filled in with this wattle and daub.

The Tudor period (1485-1560) was a time of relative peace (the Wars of the Roses was finally over), prosperity, and renaissance. Henry VIII broke with the Catholic church and 'dissolved' (destroyed) the monasteries leaving scores of England's greatest churches gutted shells. These hauntingly beautiful abbey ruins surrounded by lush lawns (Glastonbury, Tintern, Whitby) are now pleasant country parks.

While few churches were built, this was a time of house and mansion construction. Warmth was becoming popular and affordable, and Tudor buildings featured small square windows and often many chimneys. In towns where land was scarce, many tudor houses grew up and out, getting wider with each overhanging floor.

The Elizabethan and Jacobean periods (1560-1620) were followed by the English Renaissance style (1620-1720). English architects mixed Gothic and Classical styles, then Baroque and Classical styles. While the ornate Baroque never really grabbed England, the Classical style of the Italian architect, Palladio, did. Inigo Jones (1573-1652) and Christopher Wren (1632-1723) and those they inspired plastered England with enough columns, domes, and symmetry to please a Caesar. The Great Fire of London (1666) paved the way for an ambitious young Wren to put his mark on London forever with a grand rebuilding scheme including the great St. Paul's and over 50 other churches.

The Georgian and Regency periods (1720-1840), were rich and showed their richness by being very classical.

Grand pedimental doorways, fine cast iron work on balconies, Chippendale furniture, and white-on-blue Wedgewood ceramics graced rich homes everywhere. John Nash, Jr. and Sr., led the way giving the trend-setting city of Bath its crescents and circles of royal Georgian town houses. England used to levy a window tax. Even the most elegant houses of this period had bricked-up false windows — one of the earliest tax dodges.

The Industrial Revolution shaped the Victorian period (1840-1890) with glass, steel and iron. This was also a romantic period reviving the 'more Christian' Gothic style. London's Houses of Parliament are neo-Gothic — just 100 years old but looking 500 — except for the telltale modern precision and craftsmanship.

While Gothic was stone or concrete, neo-Gothic was often red brick. These were England's glory days and there was more building in this period than in all previous ages combined.

The architecture of our century obeys the formula 'form follows function' — it works well but isn't particularly interesting. England treasures its heritage and takes great pains to build tastefully in historic districts and to preserve its many 'listed' buildings. With a booming tourist trade, these quaint reminders of its past are becoming a valuable part of the British economy.

British TV

British television is so good — and so British — that it deserves a mention as a sightseeing treat (especially after a hard day of castle-climbing) over a pot of tea in the comfortable living room of your village bed and breakfast.

England has four channels, BBC 1 and BBC 2 are government-run, commercial-free and rather highbrow. ITV and Channel 4 are private, a little more 'down market', and have commercials — but these commercials are clever, sophisticated and a fun look at England.

While other countries may use TV to homogenise the way their people speak, England protects and promotes its regional accents by its choice of announcers. British TV is limited to a few morning shows after breakfast, educational shows during a midday period, and a full slate of evening entertainment shows.

American shows are very popular — especially the 'Dallasty' group, *Hill Street Blues*, *Cheers*, and *Cagney and Lacy*. Oldies like *Bewitched* and *I Dream of Jeannie* are also shown. An increasing number of Australian shows are also being seen in Britain.

The visiting viewer should be sure to tune in to a few typical English shows. I'd recommend a dose of English fun with *Only Fools and Horses*, political irreverence with *Spitting Image*, and the topnotch BBC evening news. For a tear-filled taste of British soap, see the popular *Coronation Street* or *Eastenders* and, for an English chat show, see Terry Wogan's comedy show.

And, of course, if you like the crazy off-beat fun of Benny Hill and Monty Python — you've come to the right place.

Telephoning in Britain

Take advantage of the telephone. You can make long distance, or 'trunk', calls direct and easily and there's no language barrier. I phone ahead for rooms, to check opening hours, reserve theatre tickets, and even to call home rather than mess with postcards.

The old pay phones take 10p coins. When you reach your number you'll hear the famous 'rapid pips'. Push in the coin and talk until you hear more pips which means it's time to sign off or pop in 10p more. Newer phones ingeniously take any coin from 2p to one pound and a display shows how your money's doing. Only completely unused coins will be returned, so put in biggies with caution.

Dialing 100 gets you the operator who can connect you with international assistance. 999 is emergency (free), 142 is London directory assistance, and 192 is assistance for other areas. When phoning abroad, remember to take account of the time difference. Calls after 6:00 pm are cheaper and there is no minimum time limit.

Area codes for calling long distance are a headache. England has so many area codes you wouldn't believe it. For local calls, just dial the 3 to 7 digit number. Area codes for 'trunk' calls are listed by city on phone walls or through directory assistance. Area codes in Britain and Europe start with zero.

If dialling from another country, you replace that zero with the country code. For instance, England's country code is 44. London's code is 01. My London B&Bs number is 727-7725. To call it from the USA I dial 011 (international code), 44 (British code), 1(London), 727-7725. To call it from Brighton, I dial 01 (London) 727-7725. To call the USA direct from England, I dial 010 (international code), 1 (USA code), 206 (my Seattle area code) and the seven digit number. International calls are easiest on the new phones that take bigger coins.

Telephone Directory

City	Area Code	Tourist Info
London	01	730-3488
Salisbury	0722	334956
Bath	0225	62831
Cardiff	0222	2728
Stow-on-the-Wold	0451	30352
Wells	0749	72552
Stratford	0789	293127
Iron Bridge Gorge	095245	2753
Ruthin, N. Wales	08242	3992
Blackpool	0253	21623
Windermere	09662	4561
Keswick	0596	72645
Oban	0631	63122
Inverness	0463	234353
Edinburgh	031	557-2727
Durham	0385	43720
York	0904	21756
Cambridge	0223	358977
Dublin	01	747733

Operator	100	London Dir. Assist.	142
Emergency	999	Outside London	192

Weather report, Lake District — (0532) 8092
Heathrow Airport departures — 745-7067

International code   010

Australia	61	Netherlands	31
Belgium	32	New Zealand	64
Canada	1	Nigeria	234
France	33	South Africa	27
Germany	49	Switzerland	41
Hong Kong	852	USA	1
Italy	39		

Weights and measures

These can be very confusing as Britain is only partly metricated. However, the British manage with it all very well so if in doubt, ask!

Road distances and speed limits are still given in miles or miles-per-hour on road signs, though maps will usually also give distances in kilometres. Your hire car will probably show kilometres as well as miles on its 'speedometer'.

Petrol is sold by the litre or the gallon and garages will display both prices. You will probably find it easier to 'fill up' or buy petrol by the pound, eg £15 worth.

Material and floor coverings are now usually sold by the metre but shop assistants are well used to converting for those customers who still insist on buying in yards, feet and inches. Food sold over the counter is usually sold by imperial weight (pounds and ounces), shown as 1lb, ½lb, 6oz etc. Pre-packaged food, on the other hand, is usually metricated.

And American visitors in particular need to remember two things. The British (Imperial) liquid measure is different from the US liquid measure (1 imperial gallon = 1.2 US gallons) and the British shoe sizes are smaller than the US ones.